ACCEPTING
YOUR
BEST SELF

Nancy Zimmerman

Hedgehog Hill Press

An imprint of NJZ Enterprises

NJZ Enterprises
P.O. Box 3148
Anderson, IN 46018

www.nzbestself.com

A Hedgehog Hill Press original, 2018

ISBN 978-0692536957

ADDITIONAL BOOKS IN THIS SERIES

Embracing Your Best Self

Confronting Your Best Self

Balancing Your Best Self

Dedication

I dedicate this book to a special friend whose friendship expanded my definition of acceptance, and love, even as I wrote this book. He accepted everything about me and in that acceptance showed me a love that no one else has ever shown me. I will not embarrass him by naming him, but he knows who he is. With this dedication, I hope he realizes what a special place he holds in my life and in my heart. Thank you.

Acknowledgments

I would like to thank my cover designer, Jordan Huffer, for her artistry in helping achieve what this book is meant to convey.

Another great big thank you goes to my editor, Vicki Adang. She has been with me through several books in different genres and always provides many insightful comments that add to the finished product. I found a true gem of an editor when I found Vicki. Thanks so much.

I have to acknowledge my friends who have been so very supportive of all of my work. They have provided me with a safe environment in which to grow as a person and an author. While many are no longer with me, I know that each and every one who has passed through my life has added to it in a way in which no other individual could.

PREFACE

Once we have discovered who we really are and we have embraced our best self, we are ready to begin really living life. But then our perceived reality sets in, and we wobble a bit. We begin questioning the very things we discovered about ourselves and our life. We handle some difficulties better than we used to, but we find ourselves slipping back into old patterns. We then confront those issues and learn how to better deal with them. After that, we set about the task of rebalancing our life. We apply certain strategies and take care of our vibrational energy and stand back to see what happens. This is where this book comes in.

Whatever happens, we need to accept it. Full throttle acceptance. It sounds so very simple. Let's take another journey to our best self and be thrilled by the ride. Join me, won't you, and we will jump off the cliff together.

If you have followed this journey, you started with me and saw some of the issues I had overcome—or thought I had overcome. I had placed my issues aside and was able to get to a wonderful place by reading the wisdom of many authors, by doing affirmations, by practicing manifestation to gain things I wanted into my life. I was living my life joyfully.

During this time, the friend who had been instrumental in guiding me as I questioned spiritual issues passed from the physical back to the nonphysical. While I accepted this, a big hole, a vacuum, was created, and I wasn't sure how to use my vibrations to get back to where I wanted to be. I was not grieving; I just missed her presence both spiritually and physically.

While dealing with this, I allowed myself to question other events and issues again, and before I knew it, a year had passed. I had regained some weight I had lost. I had let my house and yard become less attractive because of indifference. In essence, I had taken two steps forward and one step back. I still had the basics in my life, but I was missing the very heart of happiness. I had not yet learned that we can look at the two-steps-forward-one-step-back rhythm two ways. We can view it as losing ground, or we can think of it as a cha-cha step.

In an effort to get that sparkle back, I confronted those issues and wrote my second book, *Confronting Your Best Self*. I felt that my first book, *Embracing Your Best Self,* was written to help me. However, my readers have told me that it has been a great help to them as well because it has given them a new way of looking at things. After I worked through the confrontation, I realized that we needed to balance ourselves, and that is what my third book was about.

While writing *Balancing Your Best Self,* I became aware of the word "accept." I realized that no matter what we learn or how much we confront and balance, until we fully accept ourselves, love ourselves, and love our manifested lives, we keep ourselves boxed in. When we no longer allow ourselves to be put into boxes and labeled, we are free to be who we were meant to be. When we push the edges, we experience the thrill that life can bring us.

PART ONE

PERSONAL ACCEPTANCE

GETTING STARTED

When I speak of the thrills of life, I am talking about the everyday thrill of seeing rain hit a rock. Well, maybe a bit more than that. But once you accept yourself and all of the situations you find yourself in, you will begin to see those minute occurences in your life in such a different way that you will be forever changed. Now, let's get started.

Take a small notebook, or journal if you are keeping one, and list a few of the issues in your life that you cannot seem to shake, no matter how hard you try. Until these unresolved issues are dealt with, you will not be free to truly enjoy the life you have become a part of in this time-space continuum.

As I started to work on my list, I discovered a few truths as I read from some of the writers who I turn to for guidance. I am going to include one of these now because it is fresh on my mind and I think it is good to get the idea out there early in our discussion:

Do not see acceptance as weakness. Accepting a situation does not mean you are giving up. Acceptance simply means that you recognize and understand your current situation. Acceptance allows you to be free from the shackles of denial and move forward in life, creating a new path and a new life for yourself.

www.idanceintherain.com

Just because we list our issues does not mean we have to give up in dealing with them. We can deal with them, but doing so will be easier when we accept the way the situation is now. That is the crux of any issue we have. If you can do that, you can stop reading.

When we look at accepting the facets of our life, we deal with those we like and those we do not like. It is easy to accept the things we like without too much conflict. We may want to change parts of what we like, but overall, we can be content with those items as they are.

It is the items that we do not like about ourselves and our lives that cause us problems.

We will start with some of the external likes and dislikes in our lives because they are much easier to deal with than the internal likes and dislikes. Let's go with some easy ones. Our car or our home. If you don't like your car, you usually can only think about how dissatisfied you are with it. You don't like the color, you want a newer one, and you are always seeing cars you would rather have. The more often you send out feelings of dislike, even about an inanimate object, the more vibrations you add to your life.

You are not affecting the object of hatred, the inanimate object. It doesn't respond. The vibrations you are emitting will keep you feeling bad, so you will vibrate at a much lower frequency. Because of this, you will be more unlikely to make changes that will change your situation.

It works this way for everything in your life, which is why you need to get to a better place. You need to find features of your car that you can truly appreciate. If we do not appreciate what we have, the Universe will not give us something else because according to your vibrations, you wouldn't appreciate that either.

Now, I can almost hear you screaming, *"No! No!* I would appreciate it." You are not emitting an accepting vibration, but rather a resistant vibration. We can say something all we want, but until the feelings match the words, nothing positive will take place. When you vibrate with gratitude and appreciation, when you accept what you have, you align yourself vibrationally to receive what you want.

I have set forth desires and made affirmations since I learned about the Law of

Attraction. I began studying this concept to get more money coming into my life. I did not understand the power behind the law. I originally thought it was repeatedly being positive and making positive statements. Doing those things will make you feel better, but it took a much greater involvement in the process for me to attract what I wanted. It takes understanding and practice and resolve. You need to focus on your life after achieving your desire, all the while being appreciative of where you are. If you keep "wishing" things were different, you are not honoring the blessings you now have.

I will take you through an exercise that really stood out in my mind when it came to attracting what I desired. I found the exercise in the book *E-squared* by Pam Grout. In this exercise you pick an object that you do not usually see. You can use a purple sweater, a blue dish, or something else. For this example, we can use a feather, which is what I used.

Set this in your mind and think about it, then go about your daily living, giving the object no more thought. You will begin seeing feathers or feathery objects that remind you of feathers. You have thrown out the desire, but you have not attached yourself to it; you have not given it more thought. You have lowered your resistance to this object, and it begins appearing. When your resistance is lowered, you turn in to the flow of all good things you have set your intent upon, and those things begin showing up in your life, even something as simple as a feather. Our words do no good in the way the Universe hears and responds to you. The only language the Universe responds to is vibration.

I tried this one day as I was writing. About fifteen minutes later, I logged into Facebook. There was a picture of a feather along with a purple butterfly and a daylily. Seriously, it was within minutes of setting up this exercise. This example serves as a powerful illustration of how the Law of

Attraction *can* work. Your desire is out there. You have asked, and the Universe has all sorts of experiences waiting for you.

The reason we don't get what we want is that we think about it too much. If we just send out our deisre and forget about it, it will happen. Keep your vibrations perking along to have the frequency that will match with your desires and you are good to go. Try this exercise for yourself and see what happens.

Wallace Black Elk, a Lakota elder, says, "One of the things the old people taught me about the spirits was to never have a doubt." That is where acceptance comes in. If we can get ourselves in a place of acceptance, we are then ready to go on a rocket ride.

Another idea for claiming acceptance is in the creation of a vision board or a wish board. I have heard of people who use these to increase their ability to manifest amazing things. There are many creative ways to put our desires in motion to come to us.

To create a vision board, get a piece of poster board and several magazines. Look for things that you want in your life and make a collage of those items. Keep the board in an area where you will see it often throughout the day. Enjoy all the items, and feel the feelings you will have as if the items are already in your existence. Enjoy them *now*. They are already yours. We ask, we believe, we allow, we enjoy, we don't worry, we release it, we offer no resistance. All that is left to do is accept it into our life. That is one kind of acceptance, and it is the first kind we will talk about.

As I created my vision board with a friend, I included very few material things. I have a central configuration that represents my idea of the Universe (at least as closely as I could find it in magazines, but the IDEA of the Universe at my center is there). I used a picture of eyes, which represents my soul and my existence within that Universe. Words and phrases such a love, gratitude, feeling good, wonder, unlimited, and beautiful appear. There are pictures of friends dancing, of skin and bodies. Everything on my vision board is something I accept now that is already in my life, something I want to be able to accept, or something I want to bring into my experience at this time. I placed my vision board where I can see it upon entering and leaving my office. I feel good when I look at it because it represents *me* and my desires.

THE QUIET PLACE

A quiet peace comes to us when we accept or allow our lives to unfold in the knowledge that what we want is on its way. It allows us to live peacefully and without worry. When we forget about the desires we have thrown to the Universe, they seem to gain momentum and come to us faster because we are holding no resistance. If we hold worrisome thoughts, we raise our resistance, and that resistance will keep our desires away from us. You often hear that you have to have money to make money or that the rich get richer and the poor get poorer. That is often true because in being rich, they are accepting that their life will contain riches. The poor expect to stay poor; therefore they do. We get what we expect to get when we use acceptance in a way that will not serve us. We accept that we will be poor; therefore we are.

When we accept that we are deserving of riches, the riches will come our way.

This brings an additional caveat. Read the last sentence in the above paragraph. **When we *accept* that we are *deserving* of riches, the riches will come our way.** To manifest anything, we have to believe that we deserve to have it in our lives.

Look back at your life. Sometimes things begin going smoothly for us and we begin to question why. We are, in reality, questioning whether we deserve for that to exist in our life in whatever form we are experiencing it.

Now again, we have to make some decisions. What do you consider riches in your life? Is it the acceptance of all the things that are already there? Or is it more? Is it material things, or is it qualities? There is nothing wrong with wishing for more of those things that we think will make us happier. But you must be warned: If you cannot appreciate and be thankful for what is already in your life, you are resisting the very gifts you wish to receive. I will use another analogy, if you will allow me.

It is your birthday. Before you open your gifts, you are given a bracelet to wear. It contains a receptor chip that processes your true feelings about each gift. You receive many gifts, and the packages are beautifully wrapped. As you begin to open them, you are unaware that you are being given "test" gifts before the really amazing one. All you have to do to get that really amazing one is to be thankful for every gift you open and receive it with the love that the giver intended. This will be recorded by the chip in the bracelet. You open first one gift, then another. You thank the giver, but you are thinking, "This is one of the worst gifts I have ever received. What were they thinking? I do not like this at all." After you open the smaller gifts, the host announces it is time for refreshments, and you are not given the truly amazing gift. Because you were not thankful for the small gifts, you were undeserving of large gifts.

This is how the Universe works. We cannot pretend with the Universe. Our interaction with the Universe is vibrational. Our feelings cause us to vibrate with different frequencies. These frequencies attract things with like frequencies. When we are vibrationally aligned with our desires, they come to us. This vibrational alignment is referred to as our "point of attraction." We achieve vibrational alignment through our feelings about a subject. That alignment is not something we can fake. We can say things are okay or that we are thankful, but until we really feel that way, nothing will change in our achievement of our goals.

We sometimes are so busy looking ahead and wondering when something is going to get here that we overlook that the very thing we want is slipping in the back door. Accepting that situations will work out when they are supposed to, accepting that all will be well regardless of the outcome, accepting that the outcome is what it is supposed to be, and accepting that the Universe is working in our best interest are all forms of acceptance that we need to embrace for our best selves to shine through.

We are at our best when we are vibrating at a high point of attraction. We can get there when we exhibit appreciation, joy, and happiness. We are at our very best selves when we can look around and by our very thoughts and actions feel as though all is well.

As we focus we will receive. Being a Facebook junkie, I have many sites devoted to inspirational messages. I get the wisdom of Eckhart Tolle, Wayne Dyer, Deepak Chopra, and Abraham to name a few. When I was working on balance in my last book, I would see articles and postings that discussed the importance of balancing our lives. Now that I am in this book, I am getting messages about how necessary it is to show acceptance and appreciation for what is already in our lives. I am being given that which I need for my best self.

I will share with you how important the qualities of appreciation and acceptance are in achieving not only how we want the external trappings of our life to exist, but also how they will manifest. Is it a better home, a large bank account, material items, or the ability to be generous, the ability to do more philanthropy? What exactly is it you want? Many people have a variety of desires, but in their expression of what they want, they focus on what they do not have. The Universe becomes confused as to how to respond.

When you really decide what you want, you can then turn your wishes into affirmations. Affirmations are most effective when they are said first thing in the morning and last thing at night. The rest of the time you can simply forget them; but never question them. Be certain to write them in a way and with such precision that you get exactly what you want. By doing this, you are stating your intent and desire as the first thing in your day before anything weaves its way in to distract you. You release resistance when you don't think about it. Then by stating your affirmations at the end of the day, you focus once more on what you want.

I cannot stress enough that releasing resistance is of primary importance. You cannot look for your desire to come to you every day because then you focus on not having it. When you focus on not having something, that is what you keep getting—the absence of your desired object. You continue to attract the object of your focus. You will be led to achieving what you want when you focus on your feelings about the desire. You will set your vibrations to have a point of attraction, and that point is where your desires are. If you and what you want are not vibrating at the same frequency, you will not get what you want. This concept can sometimes be confusing, but it is a very simple practice, especially after your first success. Affirmations may be more help to us when we also use them to be our internal best self. That internal best self is what we are truly after because it will assure that our goals and desires are more easily reached. When we reach that place, all the external trappings will fall into place like pieces of a jigsaw puzzle.

How do you feel when you pick out a gift for someone and they give it a cursory look and place it aside? Maybe you send a gift and never receive acknowledgment that the person received it. When an occasion rolls around again, will you give that person another gift? Probably not. They didn't appreciate what you gave them, so why would you give them something else for them to not appreciate? That is exactly how the Universe reacts when dealing with us. When we look at the gifts around us every day with a sense of appreciation, the Universe is shaking to continue to give us things to appreciate and raise our frequency higher and higher with our vibrations.

Activity time again, and this one can be so much fun if you allow it to be. Take five minutes, look around, and write down as many things as you can that you are thankful for. It can be anything—nothing is off the table—but it must be something you are truly thankful for. If you say you are thankful for your old dining room table, and you are not, then it will not only not add to your vibrations, but it will lower them because it is turning toward resistance instead of allowing. If that old table came from a favorite aunt and you love it, you add to your vibrations. Your feelings must be authentic for them to add to your vibrations. Remember, it is not the words you speak but the feelings you feel that raise or lower vibrations. When you write your list of what you are thankful for, the items can be very simple, such as "the good cup of coffee I had this morning for breakfast" or "my new car." Just remember that whatever you write down must be something you authentically feel thankful for.

Wait two days and do it again. See if the exercise gets easier. If you are working on feelings of appreciation, it will definitely get easier. Not only will it get easier, you will think of more and more things to be thankful for and appreciative of more quickly. Continue to do this exercise every few days until you no longer need it because you are viewing your entire life with appreciation.

Gratitude is one attitude that will open the doors to appreciation. Most people think of gratitude and appreciation as being the same thing, but they are not. We can be grateful, we can be thankful, but that doesn't mean we are truly appreciative. Appreciation is one level deeper; it evokes a deeper feeling and a higher vibration.

As I consider an example, the car, we may be thankful we have a car that works and gets us around, but it may stop there. We do not look at all the reasons to appreciate this specific car. Why? We are too busy wishing we had a different car. This is the subtle difference between the two. When you approach everything in your life with an appreciation for its very existence, you will have reached the vibration it offers. When we are in the true full appreciation vibration, we experience the ultimate vibration of all that is, and that is love.

To appreciate the lessons of grief as fully as we appreciate the lessons of love is to experience total, unconditional love and acceptance. That is the ultimate vibration we all seek to emit. Appreciation allows us to reset our feelings. Let us say we are feeling very blah. When we cannot seem to get out of the doldrums, we can look for something to feel thankful for and turn that gratitude, or thankfulness, to appreciation. When we do this several times with several things, we find that the doldrums are no longer a place where we want to be; therefore, we are no longer there. We are now in a better place and are vibrating at a higher frequency; we are living a life closer to our best self than we were. This is the goal in life. This is the way we were meant to live live and enjoy our time on earth.

I am working on a different project now, and I am working with a very highly vibrating individual. When we are working over the computer on a mutual program, I can feel the energy. When we are working across a table in person, the energy is there. It feels like your best day ever, times one hundred, and that really doesn't begin to describe it. The vibrational charge is surprisingly so strong that I don't understand how it cannot be seen.

The energy amassed causes us to create together very well. At one point, I was writing dialogue between two characters in a scene we were crafting. He was working on the paragraph that followed. When we were both finished, we read it, and the conversation he wrote was the perfect response for what I wrote. The significance of this is that he wrote the response before I wrote the question. That is how finely tuned our vibrations are. With signs like this, we have no doubts about the success of the project, and that allows us to prolong the vibrations and let them fly higher.

Even as I write this, I can feel the vibrations on this work climbing. We build vibrations upon vibrations, and it doesn't matter the source of the good feeling.

I am sure you have had similar experiences only to have them fall away, and you are left wondering, "What happened?!" Such was the case for me in the above-noted partnership. After wondering where it had fallen apart, I realized that my partner had turned away from this project and his vibration dropped away. This project was not my brainchild. The vibration came from working together. When we no longer shared the experience, my vibrations went elsewhere, as did his.

That is why situations change in both work and personal relationships. The high vibration that attracts us to projects and others often just simply fizzles out, and our point of attraction is different.

As another example of this vibrational experience, consider how we feel when we interact with our pets. For those who have dogs or cats, think back to times when you were so immersed in playing with them that the rest of the world just seemed to disappear. Similar experiences might have happened when you were playing with your child as a baby or watching his piano recital or attending her softball game.

Any number of experiences can take you out of your daily routine and elevate your senses. When senses are elevated and you are thoroughly enjoying your experience, those wonderful feelings contribute to higher vibrations. **It doesn't matter how your feelings are elevated; it only matters that they are the highest vibrational frequency possible.**

Right now, my hands are skimming the keys as if I am no longer writing the words. The energy I feel when I appreciate my wonderful life can only express itself outward. This is what is meant when we talk ourselves into the vibrational vortex. When we are in this kind of alignment, we are no longer looking for something; we become all that is. We are what we are vibrating. I am love, excitement, appreciation, joy, happiness. I am all the wonderful, exciting things that the Universe is offering. We become the vibration.

When we are thus aligned, the manifestations are beginning. When we can hold this vibration, the manifestations come closer and closer, and before we know it, we begin seeing things drop into place. That is what I am feeling now. I can sense tumblers click as locks are unlocked. Before I know what is happening, the people and situations that ensure my success will begin coming to me. There is no other way for things to happen.

In my knowing this and living in this reality, I offer no resistance. When we can allow ourselves to feel so deeply and live so fully, we experience our lives as they have always been meant to be. It is a place of beauty, of sereneness in a field of unrest. We send out ripples of contentment, and the lives of others are touched by our vibrations. When we are at this place, those who come into that vibrational energy are affected by it without any realization whatsoever.

The goal is to get there and stay there. When we accept where we are and we appreciate where we are, we get into the vortex more easily.

I confess to being a fan of Alan Watts, a British philosopher. This is a quote of his that I think is appropriate for the discussion:

"This is the real secret of life—to be completely engaged with what you are doing in the here and now. And instead of calling it work, realize it is play."

When we attach our energy to the task at hand and do not look forward to what is ahead as being a "better place" to be, we will feel the ease of all situations. We accept that whatever is happening is enjoyable now, this moment. My mother liked to use the following saying frequently when it came to the topic of money: "Take care of the dimes, and the dollars will take care of themselves." I think we can use that appropriately with the events in our life. Accept the present moment, the small things in life, and our future will take care of itself. The concept is the same. The attention and acceptance of the small details now will ensure that the overall picture is the one we want.

Studying the value of acceptance, we need to take a couple of things into account. Look at your life right now. Each and every day is a manifestation of what you have drawn into your vortex. **Your vortex is basically the energy of both the nonphysical and the physical of who you are. That nonphysical is full of energy, and as you match that energy and align with it, *that* is when your manifestations match the desires you have set forth.**

Too often we perceive our situation, whatever it is, and look at it with the eye of lack, that is, how it could be better. Accept that it can be no better than it is now because there is nothing more than now. You may desire more, and you need to accept that also. We continually have desires, and when we accept that, we will have those desires unless we offer resistance.

All of our nows are just one big now. When we fight against the now, not accepting our financial situation, our health, our homes, or whatever we are not enjoying, we are fighting a losing effort. When we truly accept with appreciation any situation we enter, we open ourselves up to a vibration of acceptance that will allow into our lives the very thing we want. When we constantly battle against what we have, we are telling the Universe that what we have is not good enough. The Universe gives us what we ask for unless we are in that place of resistance. It can be a vicious circle, but it doesn't have to be. We just need to learn how to change our thoughts and attitudes so we are vibrationally in alignment with what we want.

When we can accept things that happen in our lives, we are basically releasing all resistance. I was talking with a friend a few days ago, and I held out my arm. I am very fair skinned and have always freckled easily. Add some age to the mix and you see spotty skin. I told him as I had my forearm out, "I realized years ago, when I was in my twenties or earlier, I did not have skin that tanned. I simply had to accept it." I could not get red from the sun and have it fade to a tan and build on that. I would get red, and the next time I tried to tan, I would only get redder and freckle. I accepted years ago that my skin was going to be exactly what it was and there was nothing I was going to do to change it. I avoided burning, but several years ago, I had a melanoma form as a result of not protecting my fair skin as it should have been. My skin tone is just one of many things that is what it is. Just as I had to accept that I would not tan, I had to accept that I had a dangerous form of skin cancer. In this acceptance, I removed distress from my life.

If we are in a relationship that was once satisfying but is no longer what we desire in our life, that does not mean it has no value. The value is that it was the manifestation of a dream at one time. We now have a different vibration than we had; our vibrations no longer match. Therefore we are at a different point of attraction.

In knowing this, when one person's point of attraction shifts, the shift is felt by the other partner, whether it is recognized or not. This happens in personal and career partnerships. When everyone is on the same page and realizes that things are no longer fulfilling, all concerned gain the freedom to follow their new desires.

When we think of acceptance, it doesn't mean we have to convince ourselves that everything is great when it isn't. I would still love to have pretty, tan skin, but it is not in the cards for me. Many times we decide to accept an event or stop focusing on an issue simply to make our life easier. This is what acceptance has done for me in all of the instances I can recall.

When we can accept things that happen in our lives, we are basically releasing all resistance. When we look at the mind/body/spirit connection, we see that acceptance plays a significant part. Aside from discovering or embracing our best self and knowing who we really are, accepting what our ego would like to convince us is a flaw is probably the most critical acceptance for our happiness. The ego has an entire set of circumstances it would like us to consider. The ego is necessary for us to establish our unique identity, but it would like us to feel inadequate so it can dominate our thinking. When we slowly awaken to who we are and begin to sort our thoughts and decide which thoughts we will dwell on and which we will discard, the ego doesn't want to let go. The ego takes our power. Acceptance of what is gives that power back to us.

Looking at my issue of weight/size, I can continue to make it a focus, I can adjust my focus, or I can accept what is right now, today. I have determined that for my own well-being and happiness, I will my body as it is. No other way makes any sense. I will continue to have my affirmations about my body and I will continue to eat healthy foods, but I will also recognize that accepting my body begins with an appreciation for where I am, then an acceptance of where I am. In this acceptance, avenues are opened to a variety of options that had previously been unavailable.

It is easy to say, "Oh, yes, I appreciate that, *but* I will be happier when this other thing happens." That, folks, is not true appreciation. True appreciation can only occur when we accept where we are and what we have just as it is with no conditions imposed on it. As with most things, if situations are in a place where we want them to be, it is easier to accept them. The true power of acceptance is when we appreciate and accept things when we would, on some level, like something else. My level of appreciation for my body is not yet total. I am getting closer because recently I have begun to value myself in a way that is not defined by my size or shape. I have started to shift my focus. In that shift, I realized that I had options I had not considered.

Again, when we match ourselves vibrationally with the vortex, or the nonphysical, we will achieve our desires. Even when we understand the Law of Attraction, we still tend to look at what we are missing rather than what we have in our lives. When we realize that what we have now is the manifestation of how we have been aligning as a physical being with our nonphysical entity in the vortex, we can see that to change our manifestation, we have to change our focus, thus our vibration. The manifestation is there and will come to us quickly when we align our physical energy with our nonphysical energy.

There are levels of our life where acceptance is felt in a different way. It is one thing to talk about accepting our imperfect body. It is another to discuss the acceptance of tragedy. When tragedies occur, grief often results. Acceptance of these times are critical at some point. Acceptance when the tragedy occurs is seldom possible, and I am not sure it would be desirable. When we experience tragedy, we need time to process what has happened and how it affects our lives. There are classes of tragedy also. We have world tragedies where people we will never meet are affected. During those times of tragedy, we can extend compassionate feelings without ever accepting a personal loss. We see tragedies on the road with automobile accidents occurring and can extend compassionate thoughts toward the people involved without having to accept personal loss.

There is another level of tragedy, and that is personal tragedy. We all experience it from time to time. Personal tragedy is the most difficult thing to accept, but accept it we must at some point, simply because we have no choice in the matter. Personal tragedy usually involves the loss of a loved one. Some personal illnesses would also be classified as personal tragedies, but they are of a different vibration than the loss of a loved one.

Accepting the loss of a loved one goes beyond the kind of acceptance we are discussing thus far, but because it entered into the narrative at this time, we will discuss it here. The tragic loss of a loved one is one of the most difficult things to accept. It does not matter what we believe about the afterlife; we are simply shaken by the idea that the person who has passed will never be around for us to hold again. Although it is impossible for us to accept the tragedy, we can accept the grief. We have suffered a loss, one that needs to be grieved. In the acceptance of the grief, we take the first step in healing. This is what acceptance does in almost every instance; it leads to a healing experience because it allows the pain to come forth rather than fester and create more pain.

I remember vividly the loss I experienced when my grandmother passed away. I was fourteen years old, and I was heartbroken. My grandmother was the person who gave me the most comfort and feeling of love as I grew up. Although I felt the grief intensely, I was at a stage in life where new things were happening every day, and the feelings of grief lessened rather quickly. I still miss my grandmother, and although those feelings of loss have never totally dissipated, the pain from them does not hold its intensity.

When my mother passed away, I felt as though someone had broken into my chest cavity, taken my heart in their fist, and removed a chunk of it. My pain was intense, and it lasted for more than eight months. Eventually, in the acceptance of the pain, I began to heal. It still miss my mother, but it is a nostalgic ache, not the pain it once was.

Here again, we realize that when the grief becomes unbearable, we somehow manage to switch to acceptance, which helps ease the pain. The acceptance does not ease the grief, but rather the pain of the grief. Grief affects us differently at different ages and with different people. We cannot set a timeframe for how long we grieve someone; the length of time is unique to the situation. What we can do is accept that it will take as long as it takes to do the grieving we need to do.

The positive side of acceptance is accepting those really great things in life. We have talked about accepting disappointment and perceived inadequacy, grief, and loss. Now is the time to talk about the ways that acceptance can help enhance your vibrations, help you get the life you want, and help you become your best self.

ACCENTUATE THE POSITIVE

"Ac-Cent-Tchu-Ate the Positive,"
sung by Bing Crosby

You've got to accentuate the positive
Eliminate the negative
Latch on to the affirmative
Don't mess with Mister In-Between

I will take time to review some of the basic points of the first parts of the *Best Self* series. At some point in our life, we usually come to question beliefs. Once we begin this quest, we never know exactly where it will lead. There is no right or wrong path for us to make the discoveries that we are bound to make, discoveries that we are destined to make, and discoveries that we need to make.

We delve into our religious backgrounds, whatever they may be. Perhaps you do not believe in God or a Universal Source. That is your system of beliefs, and there is no one way to believe, nor should anyone tell you what or how to believe or worship. It is all personal between you and the source of life, or higher power, as *you* perceive it. You look at the options and make decisions about the path that aligns with your belief of how you want your life to unfold. You look at some of the laws of karma and the universal laws that guide the planet. Perhaps you read religious tomes in an effort to sort out your beliefs. As you are doing this, you are beginning your journey. This is what I shared in my first book and referred to as "Your Best Self."

It is important to realize that you can't get it wrong. The decisions you make are not subject to anyone else's judgment. There is no judgment by a higher power. In my first book, I shared my journey and how I arrived at the place where I felt I could live successfully.

In the midst of looking at your life to reach Your Best Self, you discover much. I thought I knew what I knew. I found out that I only knew what I had been led to know. My beliefs about life were based only on my experiences up to that time. I had never questioned my beliefs the way I called them into question at that time. This happens to people in varying degrees at varying times in their lives. My life was no longer working in the way I needed it to work. I had met a new friend who called my approach to life into question. I had always hoped to be happy, and I saw a woman, about my age, who had undergone difficulties in her life and came out as a happy individual. I wanted to find out more so my life could be happy also. She and I talked. We laughed. We shared books and authors and then talked and laughed some more.

As I digested the words that had been written by inspirational authors, I realized that my demeanor and my approach to life were changing. I began to be less negative and was seeing opportunities to enjoy myself that I had not acknowledged before. As life became more meaningful, I began to enjoy it more. Little by little, my life changed.

I changed the way I looked at life, and my life began turning in ways that aligned with what I wanted my life to be. I embraced happiness by allowing myself to be happy. I no longer looked for other sources to validate my happiness. My happiness no longer depended on anyone else. I looked into the teachings of the nonphysical beings collectively referred to as Abraham. I found the wisdom in these teachings to be especially helpful. I read and reread, and then I wrote my first book. By this time, I thought I had absorbed what I needed to set my life on course.

When we make major changes in our lives at any time, those changes are enough to keep us energized while we are getting used to them. After we get used to the "new" way of life, we usually experience a bit of a letdown. Once the new wears off, we settle into a routine. It is a different routine, but a routine nonetheless. In the case of our thought processes, we have a history of thinking the way we were thinking; as we begin thinking differently, we sometime slip back into our old ways. When this happens, we need to readjust our direction and get back on course.

I referred to this readjustment as balancing. During the balancing process, we encompass the whole mind/body/spirit approach so we are less likely to become sidetracked. Remember that we will always be adjusting our course because our work and our path in this incarnation are never done. We entered into this physical body, and we will pass out of it. It is what we learn about who we really are that counts.

In every step we have taken thus far, there has been much introspection and much questioning. There have been adjustments in thinking both in the content and the direction. The content does not matter, and the direction does not matter. We can never "not get" where we are headed. We find those who think as we think, or we find that people think we are crazy. Neither matters. The only thing that matters as we are on our quest, our journey, or our path is that we feel better each day than we did the day before. When we are happier today than we were yesterday, we are on the right path. We still may not be even close to happy. That is okay too. When we feel a tiny bit better today than we did yesterday, that is what we are looking for. You will uncover techniques to make you happier, to become more fulfilled, and to achieve your goals. Your techniques may not be the same as mine. The purpose of this book and the others is not to train you or indoctrinate you or convince you. The purpose of this book is to help you learn what to look for and how to make your beliefs enhance your life, not detract from it.

The last division is the acceptance of everything with love and appreciation. When we come from a place of love and appreciation, we find that everything else falls into place. We no longer have to worry about anything that will come at us because we just accept it as it shows up in our lives.

One of the big questions is, "How do we accept the unacceptable?" The answer is simple, yet not so simple. "We accept the unacceptable by making it acceptable." To do this, we have to change the way we look at those things in our life, whatever they are, in a different way. We have to learn to look at them in a way that will change them into something we can accept. Sometimes this can be done through our thoughts.

Let's look at tatoos as an example. This was a topic that for years I made judgments on. I would see someone with tattoos, and I would judge what qualities that person possessed, especially if the person was a woman. I gave them the stereotypical characteristics of what I thought a woman with a tattoo was capable of. Don't ask me what the characteristics were because, quite honestly, I forget; even if I remembered, I would probably be so embarrassed that I wouldn't believe I ever thought that way. Once I had the opportunity to allow myself to view the tattoos separately from the woman, I made a shift. After I conversed with women with tattoos and found them to be fantastic women, I shifted further.

As I made these shifts, I realized that what I once thought wasn't necessarily true. If it wasn't true in some cases, perhaps it wasn't true in most cases. If it wasn't true in most cases, then I was viewing an outdated thought. If my thoughts were outdated, I needed to update my viewpoint. When I updated my viewpoint, my attitude changed. When my attitude changed, I accepted women with tattoos, and because I could accept tattoos on a woman, I no longer expressed any judgment. Through this process, I realized that judgment and acceptance are tied together in some cases, and I set about using this information to help me in other areas.

At this point, I am going to explain some things about myself. I have stated some of these things, but they are significant enough in how I lived my life previously to change my way of thinking that they serve to illustrate that if I can change some of my ways of thinking, anyone can. I lived in constant judgment of other individuals. I realize this is learned behavior. I was judged by my parents, and I patterned my behavior after theirs.

When we look at how people react to us, we need to keep in mind that it has nothing to do with us; it has to do with the pattern they have learned through observation and experience. If we are judgmental, it is because that is what our pattern has been and that is how we think things are supposed to be done until we see a different pattern. That is what happens when we begin working on ourselves. We look at those occurrences in life that cause us problems and perhaps look at them differently. Until I read that the way people react to you is not a reflection of you but a reflection of them, I had never considered that. At first, I didn't understand it, but then the more I read, the more I understood. I also found that as I stopped judging others, I no longer felt that I was being judged.

We will continue to think and behave as we always have until and unless we are given a reason not to. This can happen many ways, but there is one truth that will stand. When living with pain becomes greater than the fear of change, we will change. Until that happens, we will not change. We may see the need for change, we may talk about changing, but until we step across the fear, change will evade us. What we are doing may not be working for us, but we will continue until a compelling reason is presented to us to make a change. It is rather like living with the enemy we know rather than one we don't know. Change is often scary, and if we are looking at life changes, it can be even scarier.

My life was not working well. However, it was not painful to make the kind of changes that I needed to make to live a better and more fulfilling life and become much better personally. It wasn't as scary as I had thought it would be, but I found it hard to believe that such significant changes in my life could be made by such easy adjustments in my thinking. I embraced it and enjoyed it and tested it and loved where my life was headed.

When you are always in a bad mood, you are grumpy, you challenge anything anybody tells you, you play the devil's advocate any chance you can, and you are always up for an argument, people sometimes have a difficult time believing that you have changed. The answer to that is very simple when you are working to embrace your best self. You are letting all of those incorrect assumptions and actions fall away, and what they are observing is who you really are. You find that what you thought about yourself wasn't true either. You are also looking at someone much different than who you thought you were.

When you awaken and see that the person you really are has all the positive aspects that you do, you then begin asking yourself the same things I did in the example of the women with tattoos. You find that some of the things you originally thought about yourself are not true at all. You begin looking into the essence of who you are to find your value. You see that you were not who you had been led to believe you were; so if that is the case, then perhaps those around you have more substance to them also. The old judgments fall to the waysides, and you begin seeing others through the eyes of the Source that created you. You do not look at the visual aspects; you look beyond and beneath those things. You are looking with the common thread of love, and when you look with love, no one falls short.

This all waxes a bit poetic, but there is a lot of truth in this. As you see your best self, you begin to see the best in others. When you no longer judge, you no longer feel the stigma of judgment toward you. When you are not critical of others, the criticism they may project becomes unimportant in your life.

When you are not critical, you don't recognize criticism. You may recognize bits of criticism, but it is insignificant and unimportant in your new paradigm. As your thinking adjusts, it becomes easier to stay in balance.

There is a phrase in the Abraham teachings that refers to the vortex. The vortex is the field where we exist in the best possible feelings. It is an energy field where all of the possibilities that exist are found. When we hold ourselves in this vortex, we live in that place where our best self allows our desires to come into our lives. When we are in the vortex, we no longer live in the negative emotions and vibrations. We are at our best in the vortex.

It is easier to work on accepting ourselves and all of the events that are coming into our existence from a positive perspective. When our life is humming along and we have a bad hair day—pfft—we throw it off, and it never bothers us. If we are in a state of depression and we have a bad hair day, however, it is a major downer. The secret is to live life on the high side of the emotions and vibrations. Embracing, confronting, balancing, and accepting all are verbs at their root; they are all actions that we must take to get us where we want to go. In this case, they refer to steps that will create a life that exhibits who we really are.

Think about all of the people you associate with. Think of those people who are nice to you; is it easy to be nice to them? Of course. Think about some of the more abrasive associations. Is it as easy to be nice to them as it is to the ones who are nice to you? Usually it isn't. We can still be kind, but it is not as easy to be kind. This is how it is when we begin working on acceptance. We can easily accept many things about our lives. That is where I started, with the easy things. As you move beyond the issues that are easy to accept, you gain some confidence in the process.

Remember, too, you are not in a race. No stopwatch has been set. Time is only a construct to help us organize our lives. Becoming happy, fulfilled individuals is not subject to time. It is an evolutionary process that is practiced daily and gets easier and easier as the days progress.

You appreciate and you accept. One of the most crucial aspects of acceptance, and one that many people have the most difficult time with, is the acceptance of self. We are taught from an early age about our flaws. I should state that a bit differently. Most people are taught about their limitations from an early age. Children in kindergarten are excited about school, and they are told to curb their excitement. In the first grade, they are further inhibited. By the time I got them in the fifth grade at the beginning of my career, the creativity had been squashed out of them. The only ones who had energy were the underachievers who rebelled to the point of not caring that they were underachieving.

They had suffered brainwashing that said they were not capable of being anything other than a pain in the butt. They believed the messages they had received over and over. As adults they have hangups and problems that would not exist if their education had been a bit different before they even entered a classroom.

The message that most of us get is that we are somehow lacking. Because of this, we begin searching for answers when we are thirty or fifty or sixty, and we wonder why we have a difficult time loving ourselves. We have never been taught that loving ourselves is okay. We listened to messages given to us by loving parents and well-meaning teachers, and we absorbed incorrect data.

When we begin to search for our best self, for who we really are, we simply have to reprogram the data. That reboot begins when we allow ourselves the freedom to be exactly who we are at any given moment on any given day at any given time. When we are no longer basing our self-worth on anyone else's opinion, we are on our way to self-acceptance. For those who begin with self-acceptance, the path might be a bit easier. The interesting thing about self-acceptance is that the more dialogue we have with ourselves, the easier self-acceptance is. Even though self-acceptance has been the most difficult part of my path to acceptance, I am at the point in my life where I will hopefully be able to embrace that aspect of acceptance authentically in full appreciation of who I am.

As we discuss acceptance, we need to be aware of what we are measuring ourselves against. In truth, we should not be measuring ourselves against anything. Life is not a competition. We view it as such and make egoic calls like "this is better than this" or "that is better than that." In reality, there is no standard to which any of us needs to compare ourselves to. We are unique, one-of-a-kind miracles. How can there be anything wrong with that? How can we compare one thing to a different thing? It is like comparing apples and oranges. They both have different qualities, and those of both fruits are good. Yet, as we consider further, not everyone likes both of them. It is not a reflection of the fruit; it is a reflection of the person tasting the fruit.

Looking again at the messages of limitations, they are not the school's fault. Children get these messages from the time they are a week old in the arms of parents who love them. Schools just reinforce the limitations that started at home.

I am not faulting the home or the school. I am just explaining how it comes about that we have a difficult time accepting ourselves as being A-OK. We can't compare apples to oranges; therefore, we can't compare you to me and either of us to anyone else. We can't, and we shouldn't, but we do. We do it daily in hundreds of different ways. When we quit this unfair comparison, we can then accept our magnificence, and the final tumbler in the lock will allow us to open that door into our new life and embrace it to its fullest.

Accepting ourselves and ending our continual comparison of ourselves to others are the most freeing aspects of all the work that we will do, yet it is the one that many seem to fear the most. It is all fun, it is all exciting, and it is all a terrific adventure. I have enjoyed this leg of my journey greatly. I know I have found some of the answers, and I know I will never stop searching. I will always be reaching for the best feeling I can feel on any given day in any given moment. I know I am no longer dependent on anyone else for my happiness. I create my own happiness, and I am enjoying life on a level that I never have before. I am seeing life unfold in a positive, upbeat way, and I have embraced practices that allow me to accept only the very best into my life. I have tossed aside judgment, criticism, and condemnation in favor of love, happiness, appreciation, and joy. The days are better than they have ever been, and I am making wonderful connections with others. I have reached a stage where I feel that I have a perfect life. It may not be the perfect life for anyone else, but it doesn't need to be because it is my life and it is perfect for me.

In the next section, I switch to a format that I hope will reinforce the information by example. I also include inspirational words of other authors and individuals who have survived situations that would have been difficult to accept. You also get some questions to ponder that will help you accept situations that may present themselves in your life. We will discuss ways to accept the unacceptable as well as ways to make the best during the good times.

A MONTH OF WORKING OUT
SOME OF THE KINKS

WEEK ONE

FB/The Unbounded Spirit

"I have outgrown many things. I have outgrown relatives who gladly offer criticism but not support. I have outgrown my need to meet my family's unrealistic expectations of me. I have outgrown girls who wear masks and secretly rejoice at my misfortunes. I have outgrown shrinking myself for boys who are intimidated by my intelligence and nature. I have outgrown friends who cannot celebrate my accomplishments. I have outgrown people who conveniently disappear whenever life gets a little dark. I have outgrown those who take pleasure in gossiping and spreading negativity. I have outgrown dull meaningless conversations that feel forced. I have outgrown those who don't take a stand against ignorance and injustice. I have outgrown trying to please everyone. I have outgrown society

constantly telling me I am not beautiful, smart, or worthy enough. I have outgrown my tendency to fill my mind with self-doubt and insecurity. I have outgrown trying to find reasons not to love myself. I have outgrown anything and anyone that does not enrich the essence of my soul. I have outgrown many things--and have never felt more free."

Life is change, and change provides us with the opportunity to learn to accept those situations and events that show up in our lives and grow through them. If you read and reread the above bit of wisdom, you see just a glimpse of those things that change and thus those things we need to learn to accept if we are to find peace. And finding peace, joy, happiness, and contentment is what we strive to do. Some of us struggle with acceptance our entire lifetime. In the above passage, we see things that most of us endure at some point in our life. We are criticised, we may have unrealistic expectations put upon us, others may be glad to see us fail, or we may have friends who exhibit jealousy at our successes. We witness injustice and are the recipient of judgment. We are sometimes filled with self-doubt and have bouts of insecurity. At the end, however, we outgrow that self-deprecation and begin to look at enriching our soul. In the process of that acceptance, we find our freedom.

Week One Activity

Use this page to help you list things that you have outgrown that are keeping you from being your best self. In addition, list those things that are hindering your process. The two lists show those things you have accepted and no longer need to hold on to and those things you are still clutching onto. Be free with it. It is for your experience only.

WEEK TWO

And I said to my body, softly,
"I want to be your friend." It
took a long breath and
replied, "I have been waiting
my whole life for this."
            —Nayyirah Wakeed, poet

Our relationship with our body is rather interesting. We are born into the world and come from the free spirits that our souls are before they enter the world. Then we are in the "pod" we call our body. When we are babies, we have no concept of sizes, shapes, colors, or anything else that defines us. And, it seems, we do very well without these definitions. We move, we laugh, we eat, we play. We simply do the business of being a baby.

As we grow, those very same bodies help us maneuver in our world. We have a skeletal system that gives us our upright stature and a muscle system that helps us move from place to place. We learn to use our body to navigate the world, and we think little about it as we go from crawling to walking to running.

Somewhere along the line, some of us are told that our bodies are not working right or looking right or moving right. When we are told this often, we begin not to trust our own love of our body but rather we trust the messages that others are giving us about this magnificent structure of ours. This usually begins at a time when we are beginning to question many other things occurring in our life, and we become very confused about what is good and what is not concerning our body and ourselves.

As we grow older and begin questioning what we have been told about our bodies, it is often too late to undo some of the damage that has been caused in our lives. We have absorbed so many messages that we have decided, for whatever reason, that our bodies are unacceptable, so we become embarrassed by them and try to hide them and ourselves because of them. You understand this when you observe how other people react to their bodies and how they work and how they look.

Many people are satisfied with their body. One of two things has happened in their life. They have had people who have given them only positive messages about their self-worth, or they have processed the negative messages as messages not worthy of their consideration. The end result is the same— they have a truer picture of themselves than many others do.

Statistics tell us that by the age of nine more than 50 percent of girls have begun worrying about their body size and are concerned enough to consider "going on a diet" to improve their looks. The numbers for boys are rising. Girls are altering their looks with makeup at an earlier age. They are no longer using hair color to make themselves look younger, but rather are using it to alter their already youthful looks. They are turning to tattoos and piercings as a way to enhance their looks because they look in the mirror and somehow find themselves lacking. They work under the assumption that they need to change. They think that *they* are the problem.

It is when they begin to realize that there is no problem that they come to accept that they are good enough, they are beautiful enough, and they are worthy of acceptance. What they do not yet realize is that they need to accept themselves and then the acceptance of others will no longer be a problem for them.

Much is currently being done in the fashion industry to expand offerings of clothing for "plus sizes." The sad thing is that what is considered a plus size is simply a healthy size. The model of fashion acceptance is so far removed from the reality of the average person that men and women have a difficult time fitting into any "norm."

Week Two Activity

Take this week to list messages you have received in your life. As you do this, make notes on how those messages made you feel and how those messages shaped your life.

WEEK THREE

"Until you heal the wounds of your past, you are going to bleed. You can bandage the bleeding with food, with alcohol, with drugs, with work, with cigarettes, with sex; but eventually it will all ooze through and stain your life. You must find the strength to open the wounds. Stick your hands inside, pull out the core of the pain that is holding you in your past, the memories, and make peace with them."

Unknown origin

When you look at this quote, you see many different issues. In my case, my drug of choice has been food. Most of us have something that is referred to as a vice. When we take those to an obsessive state, we are looking at addictions. We have these issues because of several things.

I mention messages constantly because we are a product of our thoughts, and our thoughts are influenced by the messages we have received through the years that we have latched onto and believe are true. The truth is that those messages may very well be true, but they may also very well be false. The reality is that they are only what you choose to believe they are. When we change our thoughts about a situation, the situation changes.

Changing our thoughts to change our lives was one of the basic tenets of the work of Dr. Wayne Dyer. I probably got my first pinch of awakening when I read his book *Excuses, Be Gone!* It was the first time I had been introduced to the concept of a meme and how if some of those weren't true, then maybe others were not true either. Some limiting behaviors might be difficult to change, but again, they might not be. It was an eye-opening book, and I would recommend it, regardless of where you are in your life's journey.

In realizing how greatly our thoughts influence us, we can use this information to achieve what we truly want from life. We are no longer bound by what we refer to as fate. We create our own reality by shaping our thoughts in a way that will deliver what we are hoping for and what we want to come into our life.

As I wrote my first and second books, I began to realize the necessity of continuing to work on the pain in order to bring it to the light and the healing. When we accept our situation and our circumstances, we find peace in that acceptance. As we accept our situation, our acceptance takes away the power that the situation seems to impose on us.

As we work on our pain, we need to realize the necessity of being honest with ourselves. For years I did not keep a journal because it would have required that I become introspective. I would need to admit my pain. I felt that admitting that the pain existed would indicate that I was weak in some way. As I began writing, I found that in ripping that scab off, I was opening myself up to healing. As with a physical wound, the deeper the wound, the more often the scab needs to be taken off so the healing will continue. You cannot do this once and expect to have total healing. It will improve, but it takes a continued effort to achieve true healing. And so it is with emotional healing.

Eckhart Tolle refers to this in his writing as the "Pain Body." It is that which takes on a life of its own and lives within us. It becomes, sometimes, a dominant force that can keep us from being what we can be. It is a defining factor that causes our life to be stuck, or painful, if you will. The Pain Body is the sum total of those things that keep us from achieving and being the best version of ourselves. It is almost like a living entity that is separate from us yet feeds on us, sucking the strength from us. It is a parasite of the very worst kind.

I know from my writing about acceptance, the process is truly never over, even when the overriding issue is healed within me. Until then, it will be a process that becomes easier and easier to address. In the healing, the power of the issue loses its momentum and strength.

Week Three Activity

This week I am going to suggest two activities. In the first activity I want you to look at those activities that could be considered a vice. I use the word "vice" to mean any activity that causes a disruption in your ability to enjoy all aspects of life to its fullest.

Do you overindulge in any activity? In other words, do you have a difficulty with drugs, alcohol, food, shopping, gambling, smoking, etc.? These are only a few of the activities that people sometimes turn to when they are in a state of pain. If you have difficulty dealing with a repetitive, compulsive activity, you are using this activity to hide your pain so you will not have to deal with it. Even a positive activity, such as running or working crossword puzzles, can be a vice if it takes over our lives.

The second part of this activity will have you look at those activities and consider if they can be successfully incorporated into your life. Can you look at those items that you find unacceptable and turn them into something acceptable? As you work on this, be honest with yourself and introspective. Are the problems you see actual, or are they imagined? Work on your list of perceived flaws and decide which two or three are most important in keeping you from your best self. Even for the above example of running, consider a way to weave it into your life so it is not the obsessive inclusion that controls you.

WEEK FOUR

"Today, I will live in acceptance rather than expectation."

Ah, yes. We are entering the world of expectations. This is where much of the miasma occurs in our lives. We live in this world expecting certain behaviors of others, and they of us. We are then upset when they do not perform according to this perfectly written script in our minds. We do not consciously do this, but we have certain expectations of behavior that are different for different individuals in our lives. We tend to forget that they too have a script for us, one that we are unaware of. When the scripts collide and become opposed, we experience friction with and alienation from our friends and family.

I have a wonderful case in point. Several years ago I moved to be near my son and his family. They were expecting their second child, and I was pleased to be a part of this new family experience. I knew no one in the area, so it was easy for me to step in and help with the baby. I did this for a while and was happy to do it. Then I began meeting other people through activities and forging a life of my own. My grandson was getting older, and I felt he needed to be around other small children. So I extricated myself from the babysitter role, which was a role I had never anticipated when I moved.

My son had become used to my stint as a babysitter and had seen that as something he could count on. I disappointed him because I had not lived up to that expectation. He, on the other hand, was busy and had not provided me with the help I had thought he would for chores around the house, so he was not living up to my expectations either. Problems began to surface for both of us because we both held expectations of the other one that we had not voiced. In all honesty, I am not sure at the time either one of us was aware that we had these expectations, but it led to some breakdown in the relationship.

This happened about six years ago, and fallout from these misunderstandings still pops up at times. Today I am much less likely to take these personally than I was four or five years ago. Our expectations of each other were not realistic. I can now accept that he expects certain things of me that I am unwilling to give, and I can accept that I expect certain things of him that he is not going to fulfill. It is in that acceptance that we can find harmony.

Week Four Activity

As we work on accepting our best self, we need to look very closely at what we are expecting of ourselves. Expectations, more than anything, can keep us from acceptance of ourselves. List your expectations of yourself. Then put stars by those expectations that have become a part of your essence. Looking at the expectations without stars, are there some that are unrealistic at this time, perhaps because of physical, mental, or emotional constraints? Put dashes next to those. What is left will be the expectations you have of yourself that have not yet been realized. Those will be the ones you begin to work on absorbing into your daily life.

The second part of this exercise is to then write down expectations you have of others who have caused you to have issues. Have those expectations ever been voiced to the other party, or have you expected them to read your mind. To what extent have those expectations caused hard feelings?

Making these two lists will give you a chance to look at how you authentically interact with both yourself and others in a way that will not cause you to feel badly about yourself.

STOPPING TO REASSESS

I wrote the previous pages sporadically over a year. Other projects took center stage, and this book was relegated to the back burner. Just because I was not putting my thoughts down, however, did not mean I was not thinking about what part acceptance plays in our ability to have our best self in mind at all times. After having reread what I wrote, I think everything still holds true. However, in the last nine or ten months I have begun looking at acceptance in a much different way. It is one that works even better.

What if...

- We look at accepting in the reverse?
- We accept that conflict will happen?
- We accept that not everyone will like us?
- We accept that we will have days that are not pleasant?

- We accept that we are not going to please everyone?
- We accept that people are not going to please us?
- We accept that in the conflict, there will be tremendous time for growth to occur?
- We accept that everything is happening in divine time and divine order and that what we perceive as falling apart is actually working to our ultimate favor?

When we use this form of acceptance, we find that it actually reconstructs our vision of acceptance.

"One day, she decided to stop trying to fit in and embrace the fact that she was born to stand out! When she did, she was soon surrounded by the best kind of people; those who not only accepted her uniqueness but loved her deeply because of it!"

PART TWO

THE ESSENCE AND EXPANSION OF ACCEPTANCE

Acceptance of one's life is not resignation and running away from the struggle. On the contrary, it means accepting it as it comes.

This quote reflects what this section of the book is about. We began the book talking about acceptance of ourself and the situations we find ourselves in. This second part digs more deeply. We have to look at the totality of our life when we discuss any of these characteristics of our best self.

When we come to the belief that we embrace our best self, we must also acknowledge that we have to embrace our life. The same holds true for confronting. We confront not only our issues, but also the issues our life presents. When we then go to balancing, we begin to see that there is more than individual balance, and we grow into the idea that it is a whole life movement, just not a personal one.

We need to accept many things about ourselves as individuals. It is necessary in order to grow. At some point, however, the switch becomes necessary from our individual acceptance to the overall acceptance of everything. This is what this section of the book focuses on. We will take a look at situations that are common in one's daily life, look at individual ways of accepting and dealing with some of the events the Universe delivers, and learn how we can change those situations through acceptance in order to transmute the experience.

As you work through your own issues, please feel free to share your experiences with me at www.nzbestself.com. I would enjoy hearing about your successes and celebrating them with you.

ACCEPTING LIMITATIONS

In a book about positivity and creating your best self, it may seem counterproductive to discuss limitations. Perhaps it is, but we can learn much as we consider limitation. What are they, and do they really exist? Are we conditioned to see our limitations in order to find excuses to keep us from achieving our dreams?

We all have limits of some kind in our lives at some point. They are limits we put on ourselves, for the most part. I remember telling my children about limitations when they were young. Both of my children were bright and enjoyed learning. My son had little tolerance for some of the ways that other children would tease some of their classmates. As a result, he was often the butt of teasing also. Because he was bright, he often used his abilities and seemed arrogant. It was his way of dealing with the teasing.

As a school teacher, I realized that his path was going to be significantly more difficult if he kept assuming that veil of arrogance. I told him on several occasions, "You need to remember that no matter how smart you are, there is always someone smarter. Anytime two people get together, one is a faster runner than the other. One has longer hair than the other, one is taller than the other. There will always be differences in any two people. Do not think that because you are smart, there will not be someone smarter."

I think the lesson resonated with him, but it is a lesson everyone needs. In that lesson is the reverse message. The person who is the tallest may not be the one who has the longest hair. In that duo is one who runs faster, but maybe the other person plays a musical instrument better. With any two people, they each possess strengths and weaknesses. That is the way it is for ten-year-olds, and that is the way it is for sixty-year-olds.

I have a friend who restores cars. That is a skill and a passion I do not possess. I appreciate the beauty of automobiles and am amazed at his abilities. His restorations have won trophies. He is excellent but does not pursue this hobbie to become perfect. He knows there is not perfection in any skill, but rather there is always more to learn. Because he accepts that he simply wants to do the most throrough and best job he can, he enjoys every aspect of his unique talent. He has a gift, and in the acceptance of that gift, he creates the opportunities to showcase his talent. He answers questions from those interested in his work; they often sense his desire to share his love of restoring cars. This is the way acceptance works. He realizes that there are no limitations for him to simply enjoy his craft, and the Universe rewards him with the joy and success of his venture.

The title of this section is about limitations, so we will look at life from that standpoint. Perhaps you have areas where you excel, like the friend I mentioned in the previous paragraph. We can all look at areas of our life and find something we excel at. I have a former student named Jessica. If she were here, she would denounce this, saying there is nothing she is good at. I would disagree with her. She is one of the most compassionate people I know. She understands how important compassion is. She has not led an easy life, and she has not always been treated kindly by others. It is in this frame of reference we often learn the most important lessons. If we do not learn them easily, we are given events to teach us. She would share instance after instance of her limitations. This is the way many people view themselves.

When we decide to change our view of those perceived limitations, we can then create something with depth and purpose to help us achieve our goals, dreams, and purpose. They become lessons that, when properly used, set us at a higher level of vibrations.

It is interesting to listen to people and see how quickly they shrug off their accomplishments, their ease of finding friends, anything that is positive in their life. Rather they cling to limiting beliefs about themselves and shut down the flow of the good things in life. Limitations that we conjure up and collect as our own are much more evident to us than the limitations of other people. We may have people in our lives whose limitations are much like ours, but we will see them with more objective eyes. We will not even see their limitations but berate ourselves for the same things. This is because deep within us we realize that the limitation is not real for them or for us.

We can think of many kinds of limitations for this discussion. We can think of physical limitations, mental limitations, and emotional limitations. The thing to keep in mind is that they are all relative to your own situation. Some people out there feel they are limited because they can no longer run marathons. This is not something I would consider a limitation because I have never wanted to run a marathon. It is not a limitation for me.

As you are considering limitations, you can turn to the journaling you may be doing. Make a list of some of the things you feel limited in. Once this list is compiled, go through it again and mark the limitations that have interfered with living a successful life. Are any significant enough that they have kept you from a lifelong dream? If something has kept you from realizing a dream, that might or might not be a significant limitation. Look at those items that you feel have kept you from reaching a dream. Why was the limitation significant? We look at people who have physical limitations but do whatever they can to compensate for the limitation so they can realize their dreams. How does this apply to your limitations?

Limitations have no positivity or negativity in them except for what we assign to them. We assign a judgment to a limitation through our assessment. We must neutralize our thoughts to achieve a shift in our thoughts and attitudes about what we perceive the limitation to be. When we look at our lives after some of these discussions, we can see that what we once perceived as a limitation is not actually true. We have sometimes used a "limitation" as an excuse for not achieving something. Stressing limitations often gives us the excuse we need to accept a dream that is unrealized. What "limitations" are you accepting in your life? What changes in thought do you need to make to let go of these limitations?

If you are using limitations to justify excuses, then you are shortchanging yourself. You are also using those limitations in a way that others will probably recognize. If you conjure up limitations to avoid success in one area, you will probably do that in other areas.

That leads to blaming your lack of success on something outside yourself, something you claim to have no control over. Many people fall into this trap, and it can result in the death of dreams until we realize what we are doing. Until we realize that we are truly limitless, we continue to underachieve.

Now that we have begun thinking of limitations differently, we can begin to work from a different paradigm. We can use the perceived limitations to propel us to greater things. Think for a moment about a slingshot. When the slingshot is just laying there, lax and unchallenged, nothing happens. It is only when we put an object (our goal) in the slingshot, pull it back (as a perceived limitation), and then let go (dispel the limitation) that the object (goal) gains momentum. All the goals in our life work in this way.

If we wish to learn a skill, we will put up all sorts of roadblocks to provide us with surefire excuses so we can prepare ourselves for failure. We will have all the reasons why this thing did not come to fruition if we fail. But what if we took failure and limitation out of the game?

Once again, I am going to refer to one of the best books I can recommend, *Excuses, Begone* by Dr. Wayne Dyer. It lists all of the excuses we conjure up and precisely and methodically show us how to deal with them. I will not share his work; you will need to read it yourself. I will tell you, however, that reading that book changed my life. It was the first of a series of works that eventually led to my first book and subsequent projects. Once the excuses (aka limitations) were removed, I realized I could achieve anything I set my intent on.

You too can learn that the limitations you think you possess are only those that you have been conditioned to accept. Sometimes we perceive that a person is limited, but are they really, or are they limited because society has led us to believe it. We see artists with no arms and legs creating beautiful works of art by painting with a brush in their mouth. It is difficult to believe in our own limitations when we see this kind of achievement. We then come upon a vast truth. We are limited only if we choose to be limited. When we realize that our limitations are the incorrectly conceived thoughts put on us from others, we can break from the bonds of limitation.

Acceptance is having the faith that, despite the circumstances, all is well.

- Once you've accepted your flaws, no one can use them against you.
- "Once we accept our limits, we go beyond them." –Albert Einstein

REINVENTING NANCY

Acceptance is having the faith that, despite the circumstances, all is well.

Jump forward, or jump back, depending on how you look at it. As I began this book, I could not seem to get away from the idea of a crooked self-image and how I simply had to accept it as it was. The longer I worked on the book, the more I questioned what acceptance would involve. I had issues with my body that were causing me to doubt myself and my ability to positively relate to others I was working with.

I then realized, as I again searched and read works from various enlightened authors, that I could revamp my definition of acceptance. As I stated previously, *what if* I accepted that my body was not where I wanted it to be? *What if* I embraced a different avenue of working with my body? *What if* I explored options? So that is what I did. I spoke with friends who once had body image issues and asked how they handled them. In several cases, they chose bariatric surgery.

I had looked at surgery as an option at one time and discounted it. This time, however, I attended an information session and made an appointment to learn more. After six months of counseling, nutritional instruction, psychological evaluation, and blood tests, I had the surgery that was to lead me in directions that I could not have dreamed of at the time.

Bariatric surgery is not a way to immediately cure all of your body image issues. You do not instantly become the perfect size. You have to be ready to live with many restraints. The amount of food you can put in a reconstructed stomach pouch is minimal. You have to take supplements and measure food volumes for a 2-ounce pouch that was once 32 ounces.

One of the biggest adjustments I have had to make is the grief I am feeling over the loss of my best friend—food. When I previously had a problem and no one was there to help, I always turned to food. That is no longer possible. Luckily, my approach to life has changed so drastically that I do not have many problems that would cause me turn to an outside source for comfort, but I still miss the comfort that food had always brought me.

I am also facing the issue of excess skin. Having lost the elasticity of youth, I have skin that might need to be surgically removed after the weight is off. I realize that I am borrowing worries that may not exist. Perhaps the excess skin will be minimum. I also realize, as the doctors and counselors tell me, that to keep losing weight, I will have to exercise.

Never having been a fan of exercise, I decided to investigate the possibility of getting a personal trainer. As a friend and I were talking about a potential collaboration, our conversation led to my asking her what her husband did. He is a personal trainer. I sensed that I had found the person to help me. I phoned, had a consultation, and as of this writing, have had two sessions with a trainer who pushes my limits but also encourages me every step of the way. There are no coincidences.

Finding a tool, such as bariatric surgery, and a trainer were but two of the needs I required to successfully reinvent myself. I also had to find a way to change my perception of myself. Interestingly enough that came about through the back door. I had recently begun hosting a local talk show and had been contacted by an acquaintance I had met at vendor events. He is a hypnotist and had indicated that he would like to be on the show. We set a date for his appearance. In the course of our discussion, I asked if he would also be available to tape an hour-long internet show with me, and he agreed. He also offered me a session with him so our conversations would reflect a true-life experience. I agreed but had my doubts that he could hypnotize me.

The day of the session arrived, and my only concern was whether I could be hypnotized. He had done a relaxation exercise with me at one of the vendor events, and I thought I had been awake throughout the experience; I did not think I had truly been hypnotized. If you have never had this experience, you need to find a certified hypnotist. The session he led me through removed the feelings from things that had been said in the past to make me feel like I was not good enough. It was truly a life-altering experience. It was the final step in the re-creating of Nancy Zimmerman as it pertains to my view of myself.

As this book goes to publication in mid-2018, it has been about thirteen months since my surgery and about six months since my first hypnosis session. I have lost 125 pounds and have only 30 more to go. In the revelations that I have had since the surgery and with the help of friends and hypnosis, I have discovered that my issues were never really about weight. The weight was the manifestation of my thoughts of various inadequacies.

Once you deal with the underlying issues, you address your life differently, and your relationship with your "crutch" changes. You are like the caterpillar who becomes a chrysalis only to awaken to the beauty of being a butterfly.

ACCEPT—THEN ACT

"Accept—then act. Whatever the present moment contains, act as though you had chosen it. This will miraculously transform your whole life."

—Eckhart Tolle

I chose to borrow the title of this chapter from a quote by Eckhart Tolle. These three simple sentences open up an entire bit of thought that we can work around to help us accept some of life's less than desirable happenings.

We all have events that pop up in our lives that can be both unexpected and unpleasant. We usually do not foresee these events, but sometimes they are inevitable. Although we do not anticipate the breakup of a relationship, we are usually not surprised when it happens. We may have been living in a state of denial about a relationship, but if we are honest with ourselves, we usually have seen signs. Job loss happens with unexpected layoffs. Many of the events happen because of how we think about situations that are no longer fulfilling.

I have a friend in the Washington, DC, area who has been in a job that has ceased to be satisfying. He has mentioned on more than one occasion that he was refining his resume and putting out feelers for a new job. He recently sent me a message that he was going to be laid off, which he had anticipated. Although there is some stress over the financial implications of losing a job, he has opened up his life to having new, more desirable job opportunities come to him.

During times like these, if you can see loss as being something you chose and accept it as being a gift for your well-being, you put your body in a vibrational state that will not cause problems for you. When we fight against what *is* creating discord vibrationally, we stand in the way of better opportunities coming to us. My friend experienced this. He had been working toward an international educational opportunity, and within two weeks of hearing that he would be laid off, he was given an opportunity to work with a Chinese project that he had been instrumental in creating. He would be going to China for two weeks to pursue additional work on that project. What an amazing opportunity! Doors opened once some of the windows were closed.

We are often our own worst enemies. We stew and fret over things that happen. We often try to find someone to blame for our disappointing events. If we embrace those events as though they were created specifically to propel us forward in life, we find that they get us where we need to be and where we want to be. If, on the other hand, we give voice to how we have been overlooked for a promotion or how we hate our jobs, we find that we have more problems than solutions.

I remember vividly a scene in one of Abraham's books that went like this. If you are going to put a boat in a stream, you put it in and go downstream with the current. It would not occur to anyone to put the boat in at a certain place and go upstream. If you wanted to go to a location that was upstream from where you were, you would simply put your boat in at a different spot. It is that way in life. Wherever we put the boat in the water, it is to our advantage to use the current to go downstream.

I will share another tidbit from my time with the hypnotist. After the main session, he did some quick sessions while I was still in a suggestible state. At one point he had me close my eyes and picture my life in a timeline. When I described the timeline, I saw my past on the left and my future to the right. I saw the past at a lower level than my future, a line that would go from a lower place on the left to a higher place on the right. He asked me if I would like to move that slanted line so I would not be going uphill in the future. I asked if I could do that. He replied that I could do whatever I wanted to and construct the timeline in any way I wanted to.

He asked me to point to where I was now, which I did. I then reached out to the right end of the timeline and brought it down below where I was at the "now" point. I wanted a downhill effort that would give me a smooth, easy ride into the future. Just that one exercise made it clear that the unconscious self is in charge. I have been given yet another gift to see that life is as easy as we allow it to be. We have the power to change what we may have perceived as an uphill battle into an easier way of accomplishing our goals. I greatly appreciated that lesson because it put me back in a productive mode of operation.

Again, if you have a chance to have a hypnosis session, grab it! I saw firsthand how powerful our unconscious self is. The unconscious self is our protector. It processes tens of thousands of bits of information all in an effort to protect us and keep us safe. It does not know whether what we are telling it, through our feelings, is real or imagined. Use your imagination to feed the unconscious mind, and whatever you feed it will become your reality.

At one point in my session with the hypnotist, he had me close my eyes. He counted to five as he instructed me to go into a deep state of relaxation. I could hear him. He had me bring the palm of my hand to my head and told me it would be stuck there. He had me open my eyes. I looked at him and tried to move my hand. It would not move from my forehead. I saw him, I talked to him. He said he would touch my forearm and my hand would then be able to move, and indeed it did. We did two or three other exercises like that as he took me to deeper and deeper levels of hypnosis. That deep hypnotic state opened my unconscious up in a way that allowed suggestions to take root. With this new knowledge and the increased esteem that was created during this session, I came home ready to complete work that had been put on the back burner for a while, just waiting for inspiration.

DEALING WITH DISAPPOINTMENTS AND TRANSFORMING THEM

"Be willing to have it so. Acceptance of what has happened is the first step to overcoming the consequence of any misfortune."

—William James, philosopher and psychologist

I have drawn from many writers and thinkers to begin becoming my best self. One of these authors is Eckhart Tolle. If you want to see yourself making leaps into the world of enlightenment, I would strongly recommend his book *The Power of Now.*

When you combine his philosophy with that of other current philosophers, you will get a blueprint for living a more fulfilling life. He and I share many overlapping statements. I will give him credit for all of my thoughts on the subject, however, because he states them much more eloquently than I do. He is intensely keyed into the power of the here and now. His premise, and the one I have adopted, is that everything is okay *now.*

He goes further to explain that there is not a series of "nows" as we progress through life, but rather there is only one "now." It is always now. When we can grasp this concept, time falls away, and what we think of as being in the past is simply now. There is no past and no future. When we agree that this is the way it is, we see that things only happen to us now.

When we accept that, we then go one step further to agree to accept everything as okay now. If there is no past and no present, if everything is okay in the existing now, then we find that there is nothing that cannot be overcome. We only have to accept. This is the power of acceptance and how it can work for us.

Boy meets girl, boy falls in love with girl, it doesn't work out. Accept that it is okay. It is the Universe telling us that the relationship or its absence is exactly what it is supposed to be now. It is not destined to be anymore than it is right now. It is possible that it will be reawakened at another time, or it may be simply a passing relationship. It is being sent to teach us acceptance—acceptance of loss perhaps or at least the acceptance, to some degree, of defining what we do or do not need in our lives at this time. When we accept the disappointment that comes when we have a need or dream that is not fulfilled, we are opening ourselves up to the arrival of what we want. This is preparing us for the fulfilling relationship that perhaps is on its way. It is a simple premise, but one that is foreign to our egotistical way of thinking.

Our ego tells us that unless we get what we want, when we want it, in a way that pleases us, we are failures. Nothing could be further from the truth. When we look at the events in our lives with acceptance, we find that we are having experiences that are working out more often simply because we accept everything as though it is exactly what we had planned for.

If you have read my other three books, you have been introduced to some of the situations I have experienced, how I have handled them, how they have influenced me, and how I deal with them now. I will continue to share some instances in which I have had to listen to the wisdom of the teachers I have read to get to that place of acceptance. I had to trust what I have come to believe. It does not often come easily, but I find that the more difficult trust was, the easier it is becoming.

I met someone a couple of years ago who was to have a profound effect on me. We were instantly drawn to each other and recognized that we had probably been together in some way during previous lives. We worked on a project together, and when the first phase of the project was finished, he began to pull away from the energy of the work. We spent a limited amount of time to complete the project and even began a second project together. It became more and more evident that I was putting in the time and energy to finish both projects in a timely fashion. Still, even acknowledging this, I did not accept the downward spiral that our collaboration was taking.

I wanted to hold onto this person, hold onto this quasi-relationship, hold onto the partnership. Our early working experience had been so exhilarating that I was not ready to admit or accept that it was simply a short-term partnership. Because I remained attached and did not accept the decline of the collaborative effort, I continued to feel unworthy. When the work began, I had a strong positive feeling about myself and my abilities. I did not question my contribution. When I did not accept the deterioration, I opened myself up to insecurities.

Once I accepted that the work was one-sided, that I was giving far more than I was receiving, and that the project only served to provide another person with a sense of worth, I was able to detach from it. Once I detached, I looked through a different lens and saw the collaborataion for the unbalanced effort it was. However, the experience served me very well. What confidence I lost was only temporary. I picked up a great deal of experience and expertise in both areas of the project, and that enabled me to advance more quickly on my own than I ever would have had I not experienced this event. In accepting what it was in the now, I gained peace.

What I gained while I was associated with this partner was phenomenal in some respects. He served as a conduit for me to get closer to my goals. I accept that while it was not what I thought it to be, it was valuable to me. I accepted that I was doing most of the work, so I cannot fault him in that respect. We need to be careful that we do *not* accept situations where we are undervalued. When we continually allow someone to take advantage of our good nature, of our work ethic, of our abilities, we are shortchanging who we are meant to be. Accept your value, and you will not find yourself prolonging a counterproductive partnership.

We sometimes feel that we are constantly being disappointed, and sometimes we are. We are disappointed only because we hold other people up to our expectations. Now, let me clarify again what I mean by expectations. I expect people to treat me with respect because I treat them with respect. The kind of disappointment I am talking about comes when we expect some short-term behavior to mesh with our thoughts of what the other person should or should not do.

A good example is the person who says, "I'll call you." We each have a timeframe that we attach to that statement. If you are calling a business associate and the administrative assistant says she will have the boss call you, you usually think that means that day. If you hold that expectation and the boss does not call that day, you experience disappointment (and sometimes anger and irritation). Again, when you detach from the outcome, you allow the natural return of the call to take place, and you do not experience negative emotions. You made the call; the secretary took the message. It is her job to get the message to the boss, and it is his job to answer the message in a timely fashion. Accept this. Do not try to configure the when, and you will not be disappointed. You have put no limits on the conversation; you have simply accepted that it will take place. Problem solved. When you accept that it is not your place to put expectations on anyone else, you will not even have a problem to solve. If the call is never returned, that no longer matters because you have not attached to it.

There are many situations and many times when our expectations cause us a great deal of grief because we simply do not accept that we are all different with different hopes, dreams, and ethics. What works for one person does not necessarily work for everyone. When we allow and accept that some people will disappoint us, they no longer do. We have taken away their power to disappoint because we have removed the expectation.

In the situation I referred to previously, when I gave up the expectation that my partner and I were going to work on phases two and three of the first project and subsequently realized that we were no longer going to be working on the second project, I was able to reconfigure my career projects in a way that worked out better than our combined projects. I accepted the disappointment, and in that acceptance the disappointment dissipated. Not only was it removed, but the negative feelings associated with the disappointment were also gone.

Accept that you will not always see eye to eye with others. There is nothing wrong with disagreement as long as the conversation does not become disrespectful. Accept that not everyone will like you. Not everyone likes peaches, but that does not mean peaches have no value. It simply means that not everyone likes peaches. Do not take things personally. This is one of the Four Agreements affirmed by don Miguel Ruiz. How someone interacts with you is never about you; it is a reflection of the person doing the interaction.

HOW ACCEPTANCE KEEPS US
IN THE VORTEX

There's so much grace in acceptance. It's not an easy thing to do, but if you embrace it, you'll have more peace than you ever imagined.

The discourse on acceptance can be never-ending as we go over situation after situation in which acceptance proves to be the equalizer for our vibrational health. We can do several things that will keep us strumming through life at our highest potential, and that is the topic of this chapter.

The Vortex is a term that applies to that highest vibration when we are feeling our happiest, our most content, our most thankful, and our most aligned with what we want and who we want to be. It is easy to get into this state once you recognize it. I will lead you through a scenario that will illustrate how I accomplished this. You will not access the Vortex in the same way I do because your experiences are different than mine, but the process is the same.

I became aware of my vibrational health through the works of Abraham, a nonphysical energy channelled through Esther Hicks. We channel energy all the time, whether we recognize it or believe it or not. It is simply as factual as gravity. We do not have to believe in gravity for gravity to exist. We are all energy from the ultimate Source of being. As such, we all possess this same energy, and we are all connected. I am sure you have noticed people who exude tremendous energy. The tenor of the room shifts when they walk in. There are also those whose vibrations are so low that we feel dragged down when they are in our midst. That is what I am talking about when I refer to the Vortex.

When you are in the high vibrational state that aligns with who you are and what you want, you're in the Vortex. Getting to this state is our daily goal because when we are in this state, we begin allowing all that we want in life to flow to us.

If you read the works of Abraham through Esther Hicks, you will begin to understand this powerful ability we all have. The teachings of Abraham were the basis for the movie *The Secret*, which ushered in knowledge and appreciation for the Law of Attraction.

While we know that positivity is good, what I am talking about is more than positivity. We need to remember that the Vortex is a feeling. This is why acceptance of everything in our life is so important. We can be as positive verbally as we can be, but until we *feel* the truth of our words, nothing will change. This is where acceptance is crucial.

We get into the Vortex with feelings of love and appreciation. We can be truly loving and appreciative in many instances, but for those times when we have difficulty, we can turn to acceptance of all situations. Eckhart Tolle's words can be remembered here, for us to accept everything as though we had planned for it to happen. When you realize that everything that happens is supposed to happen so you can get to that place you need to be, it is easier to exhibit acceptance.

Each and every experience we have opens us up for more and more expansion in our lives. This becomes understandable when you think back to times in your life when you really wanted something. I mean you *really* wanted it. If you got it, you were happy—for a time. Later you might look back and try to remember what you were thinking to want something that ended up bringing so many disagreeable moments. Then there are times when you don't get what you had hoped for, you allow depression to enter, and you spend far too much time mourning what "could have been." Years later when other opportunities come your way, you look back on the not receiving as being a blessing. *What if*…we looked at every occurrence in our lives with acceptance. We didn't get a particular job because that job, no matter how much we thought it would fulfill us, would have been an extreme disappointment. Accept that a better job is out there, and the Universe is working to see that we get it. The relationship you had hoped for did not work out. The Universe is putting steppingstones down to get you to the perfect relationship. In both of these scenarios, the job or relationship that we get may surpass anything we could have imagined for ourselves, and it may be entirely different than we had imagined, but it was exactly what we needed.

To get into that alignment that will allow things into our lives, we need to not only show love, kindness, appreciation, and joy, but also accept all that happens in our life as part of the plan. You will attract things that are vibrating at the level you are vibrating. If you cannot and do not accept the reality of events as "okay," you are lowering your vibration, and what comes into your life will not be fulfilling. You will not be aligned with what you want. You create your reality with your feelings and vibrations. In the world of vibration, like attracts like. Accepting everything as part of the plan opens up those doors as surely as love and appreciation do.

WHY DO WE FIGHT LIFE SO MUCH?

*"The first step toward change is awareness.
The second step is acceptance."*

—Nathaniel Branden

As I write, this book seems to be organizing itself all on its own. With this kind of writing, I find that there is no reason for me to consider an outline because each thought leads to another, and both my conscious and unconscious mind seem to be able to present my thoughts better than my outlines ever can. So I don't fight it. I accept it with the understanding that it will be organized in exactly the way it needs to be for the message to be received by those reading it.

This book is the fourth in a series that I had never even contemplated when I wrote and published my first book in 2013. I thought that book was simply going to be a way for me to coalesce all of the information I had read into one volume that would combine the thoughts and terminology of many writers. Something that I could understand more easily and that might benefit others. I had no idea of the journey it would take me on and the opportunities I would have along the way. It has surpassed my imagination.

I began accepting all of the positive changes, naturally. What I realized was that while I could be positive when things were going well, I found it much more difficult to accept the disappointments that cropped up. This is a pretty prevalent feeling and way of thinking for most people around the world. We all like instant gratification, and when things do not go as we had hoped or planned, we get frustrated and oftentimes angry.

If you look at the history of the world and how mankind interacts with his environment, you will see that countries fight. We fight among ourselves, and we fight within ourselves. We have certain standards and expectations that we hold about situations. When the reality of what is happening does not match our expectation, we fight it. *What if we simply chose not to fight it?* Would the world as we know it end? Most assuredly not. The world as we know it would become even more amazing for us.

George Orwell once said that happiness can only exist in acceptance. As you come to accept more and more situations in your life as being exactly part of the plan and the path that you are undertaking, the journey becomes easier. I am going to repeat one exercise from a hypnosis session because it is significant when we look at goal setting and how we see our future.

During one of the mini-sessions, the hypnotist had me close my eyes. He instructed me to configure a timeline in my mind that represented my life. (You can do this right now, if you wish.) I viewed a line in my imagination that went from the lower left corner to the upper right corner. He asked where I saw myself, and I pointed to what I viewed as the middle. The lower part (the past) was darker in color than the upper right part (future) was. He then asked me if I would like to make my future easier. I smiled and said it would be nice to do that. He then told me to take the right end of the timeline and bring it down as far as I wanted to. I brought it down to an even mark (I literally reached out into the air and placed my index finger on where my mind had the endpoint). As I brought it to a level aspect, he asked if that was as far down as I wanted to put it. I replied, "You mean I can take it lower? I can make the rest of my life even easier?" He responded that I could do anything with the rest of my life I wanted to. I could make it as easy or as difficult as I wanted it to be. I took that line down even farther so I would have a comfortable ease to my life from my present to my end.

If you did this in your mind, you will see that life can be that simple if we accept that it is that simple. When we quit fighting our bodies, quit fighting our financial situation, quit fighting our professional situations, then in that field of acceptance, everything opens up to our best advantage. If you are shaking your head and disagreeing, that is okay. I will say this to those who are in that mind-set: Accepting your life as it is does not mean you have to accept disappointment. You do not have to accept anything less than what you want. I will share the following bit of wisdom. I cannot claim credit for it, but it has been extremely valuable as I have worked on acceptance.

- Do not see acceptance as a weakness.
- Accepting a situation does not mean you are giving up.
- Acceptance simply means you recognize and understand your current situation.
- Acceptance allows you to be free from the shackles of denial and move forward in life, creating a new path and a new life for yourself.

Those four statements can provide a powerful impetus for you to take a current situation and propel it into the future with a great deal of momentum to make the changes you need to make.

I AM OKAY

"Acceptance does not mean you agree with, condone, appreciate, or even like what has happened.

"Acceptance means that you know, regardless of what happened, that there is something bigger than you at work.

"It also means you know that you are okay and that you will continue to be okay."

—Iyanla Vanzant, inspirational speaker

I originally titled this chapter, "I Will Be Okay." I realized in doing that, I was projecting the belief that I didn't think I was okay now. Because that was not the case, I rewrote the chapter title. When you go through your daily life and restructure your thoughts and actions, that is what you need to become aware of. It is in our thoughts that our dreams and goals are realized. We can misthink something, but when we realize we have done so, it is imperative that we reconstruct those thoughts.

This brings us to another subject that I covered extensively in my first book and has been written about by many authors who have been at this kind of work far longer than I have. There is a power to the words "I Am." Whatever follows those two words sets an intent with the Universe that will be matched by the frequency of the words that follow it.

I used to say, "I am sick and tired..." of whatever. As a result, I found myself worn down and bedraggled with the events in my life. The Universe gave me more to be sick and tired of because that was what I was continually focusing on. I no longer get sick and tired. I may think, "I am looking forward to some restful alone time..." or whatever it is, but I phrase it in a way that does not detract from my appreciation and acceptance.

This quote probably shifted the focus of this book more than anything. As I began writing, the focus was on learning to accept the unacceptable. I still believe that we need to be able to do that. I see now, however, that even though we may find some things unacceptable, if we realize that we are okay with them just as they are, we are accepting them. So we accept the unacceptable, knowing that it is leading us to a greater understanding and awareness. Accept it knowing that it is part of the journey, it is preparing us for what lies ahead, and we will survive the experience.

How we survive the experience depends on the degree of acceptance we choose to give it. I say "choose" because all of our reactions are choices of how we will respond to any given event or situation in our lives. When we accept, we are choosing higher frequency responses than when we choose anger or bitterness. The higher our vibration, the more closely we are aligned to those things we want in our lives. This is how life works for us, and we are creating our reality (what we can see, hear, taste, smell, and touch) through our thoughts and our focus. When we focus on something good and we are feeling bad, the vibrations do not match and that good thing will not come to us. We are resisting it by our vibrational difference. When the vibrations are higher, they are more closely aligned, and our point of attraction is higher. That is when the magic happens and all of life begins to fall into place. Sometimes our wishes and dreams come to us slowly, unfolding as the petals of a flower in spring. Sometimes an answer pops up in front of us without our even realizing it.

The secret for a happy life is to take all of those surprising gifts and view them through the eyes of your soul rather than the physical you. When you do that, you see those gifts in a beautiful way. Again, when you accept all the events in your life as gifts from the Universe and do so with appreciation, your life expands further and further.

I will give you an example from my life. I was co-hosting a radio show with a business partner. When the time rolled around for us to sign another contract, he told me that he would not be signing because he was going to pursue other ventures. I was crushed and had to decide what to do. I enjoyed my stint as a talk show host, but my surgery was looming, and I was not sure how long that would keep me from working at full speed. I had thought that my co-host would be able to carry some of the load while I was out. I considered keeping the radio show, but there were just too many factors for me to consider.

I had my surgery, and my business partner became less and less available discuss another major project that we were scheduled to work on. Then I realized that an online magazine I had been contributing to monthly had been trying to get me to do an hour spot on their newly launched online radio. I decided to pursue this and fashioned a show that would be eclectic in its presentation because this was a worldwide platform and had to appeal to many different cultures.

The show began in the summer. People stepped in and recorded shows with me, and I met a man who had spent thirty-plus years in radio and wanted to keep doing it on a much smaller scale. He and I teamed up, and we both remarked how we missed working in an actual studio. It then occurred to me that I could do a shorter version of a local show and format it to be what I wanted it to be without compromising the content as I sometimes did with my partner.

By this time my partner had disappeared, and I was on my own as executive producer and program director. My producer was helpful and willing to co-host when needed. The man who had helped get both shows going had a stroke and passed away after one day of taping a show on location.

I give you this example because in the course of a year, I lost not only a show, but two players who had been part of that show. In accepting this, however, I gained two shows, did all of the background prep for the defunct show and the two current shows, and got even more efficient at juggling guests. I gained a producer I was able to work with very well, and I also got to know other producers in the studio. The new shows were gaining momentum.

Had it not been for my business partner's abandonment, I would never have known the level of success I began to achieve. Had I mired myself in the loss of him and the loss of the first show, and had I not seen the upside to the chaos, I might never have had the other opportunities.

Additionally, while the online show was not to be pursued earlier, it was waiting for me when I was ready to accept it into my life. Not all things wait for us, but luckily, this opportunity did.

Another interesting thing happened as a result of the business partner backing out of the scene. While I had been interviewing guests and coordinating the show, I had spent some of my time writing children's book. He indicated he wanted no part of that particular endeavor, so I continued that on my own and re-established my own business. The books took off after several months, and ideas came for other books. After I was fully away from the partnership, the small publishing imprint I had started before meeting my partner flourished.

I tell you this because even in the turmoil and disappointment of losing a partner, I realized that he had never been a partner in the true sense of the word. He had been a partner only on paper. When you accept the unacceptable, worlds open up. You see that the way you are treated by others has nothing to do with you but everything to do with them. You learn more and more from each unacceptable situation that you accept.

Then, when you accept the unacceptable situation and release any feelings of disappointment, anger, or sadness, you are given the gift of peace. The Universe rewards you in numerous ways, some large and some small.

This gift allows you to see the reality of any situation as it truly is, not as your mind has built it to be. You see your own strengths and weaknesses and how you contributed to the overall interaction. You realize there is no blame to be placed, no feelings of resentment or anger to be experienced. You detach from the situation and view it objectively, seeing that the partnership offered many opportunities to both parties. One of the members turned from it, and the other member embraced it.

There will be times that you turn from opportunity (as I did when first presented with the online radio opportunity) because the timing is not right. We often find ourselves in situations that don't work out because the timing is not right. They may work out amazingly well at a later date, but we cannot stall our lives waiting for the timing to be perfect. If we live in a state of high vibration, those opportunities will continue to hover and be there for us when the timing is correct, or other greater opportunities will be afforded us.

As I worked to reinvent myself, amazing lessons and opportunities were afforded to me that I never would have thought of wanting. The Universe delivered the people, the places, the timing, the resources, the talents, and the energy for me to take on these projects. I have a freshness for opportunities that did not exist in me forty years ago. It has given me a fresh approach to life in both my mental and physical well-being. I am awakened, aware, and accepting in life, and it benefits me daily.

STRUGGLING
WITH SELF-ACCEPTANCE?

"Loving ourselves through the process of owning our story is the bravest thing we will ever do."

—Brene Brown

Self-acceptance is the key to loving yourself, and I still do not have that down well, but I am okay with that. This, too, is an example of what I have been saying. In the acceptance of self, we realize we are good just as we are. There is nothing wrong; there is nothing better; there is simply the uniqueness we bring to the Universe that is totally and completely ours.

I find great enjoyment in going out and looking at the night sky. The magnificence that can be found there intimidates some people and makes them feel insignificant. It does just the opposite for me. It gives me a greater sense of worth and power when I see that in all of that magnificence, *I am needed*. No one anywhere else on this planet or in this massive universe can do exactly what I can do. If I were not needed, I would not be here. To be here means we are important, we have a purpose. When we leave, we will go to other places, but we will leave our marks, whether good or bad. We will leave remnants of our energy for others to gain strength from.

A great deal of our ability to accept ourselves comes from the atmosphere in which we were raised. Sometimes we blame our parents for our difficulties in life when they don't deserve it. Most parents do the best they can with the knowledge they have. They look to those around them for clues, and they rely on how they were raised.

I was raised with a lot of expectations, by my mother in particular. She was raised by an alcoholic father, and her approach to parenting reflected that. She had no control over the home she grew up in, but she was going to control her home as an adult. Control was the main focus. I was not a child who came into the world ready for control. I evidently had my own ideas about what my life was going to be from the beginning. The problems came about when the two worlds clashed. I had no delusions of perfection in my life. I was okay with less than perfect. Mother had perfection as her benchmark, so I always failed to live up to the expectations she had for me.

During these formative years, I learned that there were some things my mother had no control over. The kind words of others let me know that I was intelligent and I had pretty eyes, pretty hair, and a pretty smile. Taking all of those plusses with me through life has served me well. The things I received from my parents, however, did not. I became convinced that no one could love me as I was and that I needed to keep trying and to be different from who I was. It led to some major insecurities when it came to relationships, insecurities that I still struggle with more than forty years later.

Within the last two years, I have realized that acceptance is never about external looks. It never has been. I wasted many years worrying about looks, thinking that my appearance decided whether someone would love me. Gaining the acceptance of others has never been about anything other than authenticity. When we authentically present ourselves to others, we are rewarded with their authentic side also. The people we see and choose to associate with are those who resonate with us because we are reflected in them and they are reflected in us. That is why the saying "Birds of a feather flock together" holds so much truth. We are attracted to groups who reflect our thoughts and beliefs. That is the authenticity we strive for.

We can be fooled by those who present themselves one way and we later find out that what we saw was not a true representation of who they were (unless, what we saw was the truth and the thought of being authentic was so terrifying for them that they ran back to past behaviors).

I recently had a man who I thought had been a close friend go from working with me to not even speaking as a courtesy. The change in our relationship leaves me totally baffled. The last time we spoke, things were well between us. Then a snub of not even speaking when the person he was with spoke to me and was congenial. He acted like he did not even know who I was. This is the kind of situation that would have brought up old insecurities in the past. Now I simply wonder what happened to him that caused him to react in such a way. It reflects who he is, and I wonder if he realizes that others observe this behavior and comment on it.

This is yet another example of things that need to be accepted. Although I do not accept the behavior, I accept that I will be okay despite the behavior he is exhibiting. Nothing is going to drag my frequency down to his. When we meet people, we are usually at the same energetic frequency level. This being the case, I can only surmise that my erstwhile friend has had some event or association in his life that has caused his vibrational level to be out of sync with mine. When this happens, relationships will literally vibrate out of our arena. Some friendships, therefore, are not long term. They last only for a certain purpose in our lives, and then we accept the loss and move on. If we attempt to hold onto relationships that have reached their expiration dates, we lower our own vibrations because of all of the negative messages we give ourselves over this loss. We begin assigning blame as to why the relationship ended. Perhaps it ended because it had served its purpose.

Accepting these kinds of events in our lives leads to a better understanding of ourselves. At one time I would have given my focus over to the demise of this relationship. I am not going to say I did not give it some thought and some focus for a while, because I did. However, I did not obsess over it, and I did not give it undue attention. I discussed it with two or three good friends because I found it so baffling. I was not angry and did not try to put any blame on him. That would serve no purpose. I vented, and then I detached and released my confusion and disappointment. I found in the process that others had seen sides of him that I had not seen. They were not as surprised as I was by his behavior.

In the acceptance and the release came the peace. I had more time for other more authentic friends. I had more time for my work, for achieving my goals and creating my success. I had more time to grow in my awareness and to experience activities that would lead to a higher vibrational frequency. I attained a shift that would have been much more difficult had I still been in that relationship. I accepted that all is well, and it is.

ACCEPTING DISAPPOINTMENT

"When yesterday was a disappointment and today isn't any better, remember there's always tomorrow, so make it something to look forward to and smile."

—Unknown

Disappointment is defined as "the feeling of sadness or displeasure caused by the non-fulfillment of one's hopes or expectations." When we cast our expectations onto someone else, we are setting ourselves up for disappointment. When we hold someone or something else responsible for our happiness and fulfillment, we are setting in motion the very things that will cause us disappointment.

Our happiness and our contentment rely on our ability to accept what is. We can certainly have hopes and dreams; it would be a very disappointing life if we did not want things over and above what we have. When we realize that what we have is truly enough and we appreciate what we have, we are given more to appreciate. We accept that we have no control over when and how we get our life's desire.

If we dwell on the how and why of what we want in our future, we experience disappointment when it does not come to us. There are degrees of disappointments also. We have the disappointment of missing a bus so we can get to work. Then there is the disappointment of a relationship that doesn't work out as we had hoped. But within these disappointments lies the germ of success. Perhaps if we had caught the bus, we would have been placed in a time frame where we would have encountered an accident of some kind. Perhaps in the disappointment of a relationship gone awry, we placed ourselves in a better circumstance for a better relationship.

This is how we gain our momentum and get into that better place of higher frequency.

We all experience disappointment, heartache, and unrealized dreams, and we have spent much time dwelling on the situations that resulted in these feelings. We replay them, and in that instant replay, we relive them and experience the negative emotions associated with them all over again. When we take a step back and look at the actual situation and how we put our hopes and expectations into it, we realize what we have done and how we have set ourselves up for that ultimate disappointment.

We need to reprogram ourselves. When we reprogram our responses, we take the power away from individual situations that throw us in a tailspin. We regain control by giving up control. We attain a peaceful solution by accepting the responsibility for projecting certain behaviors in certain situations. For example, when I see that there is going to be a problem with my children and I can shift and readjust my hopes so I do not expect my children to behave in a certain way, my day will go much more smoothly.

This can be demonstrated by how we perceive children and expect them to clean their rooms. We like our homes to look a certain way. We work with our children and teach them how to clean their room in the way and time that we like. We then ask them to clean their room one day and think that because we have asked, it will get done. How many times have you been disappointed with your children because they didn't get the job done or didn't do it as you have shown them over and over? Many times, I would imagine. That is but one brief look at disappointment. We expected certain behavior out of them, and when we did not get it, we experienced disappointment.

The question then becomes, how do I avoid this? The answer is really very simple. You simply do not expect anything of them. That does not mean they are not expected to clean their room; it simply means you do not expect them to conform to your plans and expectations. If they clean the room, it will be in their time frame and in their way. When you accept that as being okay, the problem will be solved. Expect nothing to be as you plan for it to be and you will not be disappointed.

You have a choice in every situation as to how you are going to process it. I have changed greatly over the years. I used to be disappointed all the time because people did not adhere to my schedule or sometimes the schedule they set. My daughter would tell me she would arrive at a certain time from an hour away for a Sunday meal at my parents' house. She would not be there when planned, so we would wait on her, the food would get cold, and she would breeze in at her leisure. One year, after getting tired of waiting on her, we started the meal. When she finally arrived, she was offended that we ate without her. That was how we handled our disappointment; we chose a time and stuck to it. She then chose to be disappointed. Twenty years later, my daughter will still say she is leaving at a certain time. Because I now live four hours away, we configure the travel time, I allow for travel contingencies, and she still arrives later than expected. I know this is the pattern, so I am no longer disappointed or frustrated by the situation. I shake my head in amusement most of the time. I only care that she arrives safely, but I don't know how someone can consistently be so late. It mystifies me, but it does not disappoint me.

When we change the way we process our thoughts, we begin to accept what was previously unacceptable. We turn away from disappointment. When we do this, we elevate our vibrational frequency. This becomes important as we navigate through life because all of life is based on this positive frequency. If we stay in lower frustrated frequencies, more and more frustrations will find us. When disappointment and frustration are taken out of play, little will disappoint us.

It is a process and it takes some practice, but the results are worth it. When I removed the need to control my daughter's arrival time, it got me a step closer to changing my vibration. When I looked at the situation objectively and asked myself, "Why is it so important that she arrives at a specific time? What is gained by that?" I realized I was using the situation to control my own agenda. It was an egoic need of mine to be in charge. When I accepted that my behavior was a control mechanism and released that need, I also released that need to control in any way. I still believe that when people create schedules, they should be adhered to. I probably always will feel that way, but I no longer judge those who do not hold true to that stream of thought. I do not take it personally when someone is late. It is not about me. It is about them.

I mentioned other kinds of disappointments also. There are disappointments in relationships. I was recently in a relationship that would take a friendship to a deeper level. We agreed to move forward with the relationship with the understanding that it was a tentative action on both of our parts and we valued the friendship above everything else. We did not pursue a deeper intimate relationship in the conventional way, but we ended up with a more intimate friendship than an affair would have afforded us. We both have a friend in the other who is unique and treasured. Was I disappointed? Yes, if I had been holding out for something specific and it had not been realized. I saw what was right in front of me with this person and realized the value of his friendship over and above anything else. I am thankful every day to have him in my life, and he is thankful to have me in his. We fill a niche that no one else can, and that makes it very special.

Disappointments are always waiting to pop up and grab us. With practice, you will be able to acknowledge that someone or something has disappointed you without giving it so much focus that it will bring your vibration down. It is always better to acknowledge your feeling rather than tamp it down. Denying a negative feeling only lets it burrow its way deeper and deeper to affect you later. Instead, acknowledge it and let it go. Accept that the situation is not what you originally had hoped, but look at it in a new way and see its beauty.

You didn't get the job you had hoped for? Yes, you will be disappointed until you realize and accept that you would not have enjoyed that job as much as the one you will ultimately get. Keep looking and know that the perfect job for you is out there. Put a smile on your face, and the positivity will attract what you need to help you get closer and closer to your dreams and goals. Accept the disappointments, change your thought processes, and you will be on your way to being your best self.

We always need to smile through whatever we are experiencing. There is nothing that cannot be made better by the addition of a smile. It opens you up to positivity. It is also impossible to frown and smile at the same time, so if nothing else, smiling will keep the frowns from showing up on your face. Always remember to smile.

BE A REALIST AS YOU DREAM

"Don't spend time on beating on a wall hoping it will transform into a door."

—Coco Chanel

Truer words have never been spoken. This is an issue that needs to be addressed as we discuss acceptance of all things. We often project what we want things to exist as rather than what they actually are. This is important. We create our lives through our thoughts. What we currently experience, however, is the result of what we have thought previously to bring into our now. For us to act as though something is different than it is will lead us once more to disappointment.

The above quote pretty well sums it up. We cannot treat some things the same way we do others. We cannot expect that a wall will become a door. We can, however, see that an opening can be constructed in the wall, thus allowing access either in or out of a space. In this way we can use the quote to our advantage.

When we look at situations in our lives, it is the very thoughts we give them that help us understand how they can help us. If we do not have the ability to see things differently, we will overlook the fact that, though they are different, the door and reconfigured wall can serve the same purpose—entry or exit. It is this way with many events and situations in our life. They can be used as springboards for different ways of thinking about subjects. And sometimes adjustments have to be made, as in the case of the above-mentioned wall.

If we have a job we do not like, it is imperative that we either find a different line of work or we find a way to transform that job into something we can enjoy. This is never an easy task, but it is rewarding when we are successful. Many times what we dislike about the job is more about us than the job. This is especially true if we are working at a job for which we have gone to school and learned how to do. We have put time, money, and energy into gaining the necessary skills to perform this job. When we become disenchanted, we cannot assign blame to others and none to us. Everything we achieve and gain in our life is a direct result of our vibrations. If your job has become rote and mundane, it is because you have probably lost some of your original momentum also.

This is not to say there are not jobs where a change of administration brings factors into work that were not there. The people you work with or the job itself may change. When situations morph into something less desirable, we must look for the redeeming features of the job or the people we work with. When we can keep our vibrational offerings high and look for the potential that is around us, the job will change into what we want and need it to be.

I have a friend who works two jobs and spends about eighty hours a week working. His attitude is amazing. One of the jobs is a very physically challenging job, and I know he is tired when he goes to the second job. He always tells me how thankful he is that he is working and not out looking for work. He accepts that with this kind of schedule he will be tired. He also accepts that to have the life he wants, he needs to work at this pace. He is also fortunate that both of his jobs are in fields of his expertise and training; therefore he really enjoys them both. Even during the days that are chaotic and extremely hectic, he is doing what he enjoys.

This is the kind of mind-set we need to have to be able to shrug off the lower frequencies that sometime try to creep up on us. I might add that this man is sought out for his expertise, he is well thought of because he keeps an upbeat attitude, and he has worked at both of these jobs over a lengthy period of time to gain the expertise necessary to answer questions and be of value to his employers. This is a man who life treats well and who will continue to achieve his goals and dreams.

When we consider that we can create our lives in the way we want them, there needs to be an element of realism involved. I had a discussion with a friend about this very subject. We were discussing the millennial generation. I am not sure what group that entails, but it seems to be the twenty-somethings who were born near the turn of the millenium. My friend thinks we are doing this new generation an injustice by telling them they can do anything and be anything because they simply can't.

I can't help but disagree. Through the work I have done in the last five years in my own life coupled with some of the amazing books I have read, I think it is possible that they can do what they want, provided it is realistic. If a child wants to become a doctor, they will find a way to attain the education and funding to make it happen. If they begin early and develop the skill set, I think it is achievable. If a young adult wants to become a singer but cannot carry a tune, the job will not be easy, but they will find a way if they desire it badly enough. It is an achievable goal. If they add that they want to be a famous singer who wins a Grammy, even more work is needed.

Here is the rub, however, when we look at something like that. If a girl were to decide she wanted to be on an NFL football team that went to the Super Bowl, that is pretty close to impossible right now. But there is the potential that rules could be changed and that could happen. I remember a story about Hillary Clinton when she wrote to NASA and wanted to be an astronaut. That was not a possibility for her at that time; now there are no limitations for women in the space program.

The one and only component we have to remember about achieving our goals is that the person who wants to do something, whatever it is, must believe it is possible for them to achieve it, regardless of what anyone says to the contrary. We constantly hear of people who were told they would never walk participating in marathons. We see people with no arms painting using their feet to hold the brush. We hear of incredible feats that are accomplished against the odds because the person doing it believed they could.

When you believe you can do something and it is your intent to accomplish that, the Universe will put into motion what needs to happen to achieve it. When you are tuned in to the frequency of achievement and are offering no doubt of resistance, it will come your way. One of the best books I have read on the subject is *Ask and It Is Given* by Abraham and Esther Hicks. It deals with the more spiritual aspect of achieving our goals. Once we ask, whether through prayer or meditation, our part is over. We simply need to relax and know that our request will be granted in its own time and place and manner. We are given the essence of our desire. If we pray, for example, for a specific job and we do not get it, we feel our prayer has not been heard or God has not answered it. What we are saying is that it was not coming to us as we had hoped and planned. By this time we are frustrated and upset, and our thoughts are all over the place.

If you can use acceptance to get you through these kinds of experiences, those experiences will change. Here is where the expectations and disappointments will creep in if we allow them to. You ask for a job. You don't get the job. All that means is that you did not get that job. It is not a personal reprimand from the almighty that you are unworthy. We have to change our mind-set if we want to get where we want to go. We have to accept that it will not happen overnight and we cannot take it personally.

We are energy. We are pure potential capable of amazing things. We have it within us to create the life we want. Those are all truisms. We are put here to create, to help expand the Universal Source energy. When we experience life, we add to our uniqueness. We are the way that the Source can have a physical experience. When we doubt our abilities, we send messages that block us from receiving the full benefits of being a part of that source. Just as we try to put God in a box and a meaning of our making, we do the same thing to ourselves. We have no idea of the true magnificence of who God is and of who we are. It is boundless. All we have to do is accept everything as it is given to us knowing that it is serving to get us what we have asked for.

My son would be quick to point out about now that I have slipped over into the land of the "woo woo," but that is okay too. I don't take it personally. I know that turning my thoughts around and learning to accept life as it is now has opened up paths that I had never dreamed of previously. That is what I am hoping this book does for you. My thoughts did not change overnight. I began adjusting my attitude many years ago. I saw that others had lives that seemed charmed, and I seemed to struggle. I had strengths, but I saw only my flaws and my weaknesses. I found it difficult to take a compliment. I wondered if it was a sincere compliment or if someone wanted something from me and was using flattery to get it.

When you begin to realize that we are simply vibrational beings and attact things of like vibrations, you will begin to attract those things into your life that you desire. There are steps to get there, and one of the biggest doors to open is that of acceptance. As in the case of the job we didn't get, when we accept that it was not in our best interest to get that job, we are already in a better place to receive the job that is waiting for us.

ACCEPTING OUR DIFFERENCES

"It is not our differences that divide us. It is our inability to recognize, accept, and celebrate those differences."

—Unknown

Learning to accept the differences in individuals is paramount if we are to gain access to that higher self, that best self. There are many differences between us and other people. Some of those are easier to accept than others. We also must realize that when we are discussing differences, there is a great difference between acceptance and tolerance. Many think they are the same, but vibrationally , they are very different. If we are going to create a world where we exhibit our best self, we need to be aware of the differences.

Tolerance takes place when you make an observation and think, "I can live with that." It may be something that you don't really care for, but you know you are unable to get it out of your life, so you adjust yourself so you can live through the experience.

Acceptance, on the other hand, is something much deeper. It is looking at a situation with approval and endorsement, saying not only can I live with it, but it is okay in my life. I will enter into friendships and relationships with these people who have different ideas.

Acceptance is what we strive for as we navigate through life with those who are different from us. When we look at the vast array of more than seven billion people on the planet, we realize that within this miasma each one is different. There are defining factors within these differences that will group some together in a way to make them seem similar. We group according to nationality, country of residence, race, gender, and many other ways. As we then look at the groups, we find ourselves sorting out those we accept and those we merely tolerate.

The goal is to find all groups acceptable. When we are in a different country with different customs, we find that experience interesting. We pay for the experience of the difference when we travel. Some, however, look at visitors and immigrants with those same customs in our country with disdain and sometimes even hatred. Sometimes those immigrants are only tolerated. They are deemed unworthy of our attention and kindness, but we do not go out of our way to do them harm. We simply tolerate their presence.

When we accept them into our country or our lives, we look for ways to include them in activities. We learn about their foods, their customs, and what makes them unique within their group. As we accept the group, we get to know the individuals within the group. As in any group of people, some individuals will resonate with you more than others do. It is not for us to simply tolerate any; we accept that all are different, and those who do not fit with us vibrationally will not become part of our circle of friends. We can still, however, treat them with kindness rather than disgust or antagonism when we are around them.

I have always enjoyed the diversity of people around me. I find their stories to be fascinating because they are so very far removed from my story. Their experiences in a different culture evoke different foods, arts, music, clothing, language, and customs. They add to the tapestry of the world, and they enrich my life. I accept the group, and I enjoy getting to know individuals from the group.

I do not mean to imply that I accept each group of people as easily as the next, but I try to look for the best parts of each group and focus on that. It is not going to change anything if I focus elsewhere. I do not like to merely tolerate people. There is a negativity in toleration that does not make me feel good. It is like a cloud hanging over me just waiting to start a downpour of lower frequency.

Differences exist within families. If you have brothers and sisters, you can see the differences between them. These are individuals who share the same parents. If those who share the same parents can be so different, then how can we expect others not to exhibit differences? Rifts often occur in families because those differences are not acknowledged and accepted. We place certain expectations on close family members that we do not impose on friends. We then wonder why everyone does not get along.

Until we truly accept the differences among people—whether it is our brother or sister in our own home or our brother and sister from another country—there will be times of discord. This is only a brief look at differences as they apply to customs and countries. There are differences that are even more subtle that people have a difficult time accepting.

Within each country there are differences in heritage, dialects, religions, and politics. For some, even age poses a reason to be intolerant and unaccepting. I use both terms because they are both applicable. When we look at differences, many people deny that they are biased or prejudiced against any one group. You only have to look at how the elderly are treated in this country to see that is not the case. When an older person is walking slowly or in a wheelchair, some people give off an air of barely tolerating the person. They are anxious for the older person to move out of their way and do so quickly. They are intolerant and unaccepting. You then have the people who tolerate it, but you note that they dislike being slowed down by their pace. Then there are the accepting individuals who may open the door to help the person rather than scorn the fact they are moving slowly.

The differences between tolerance and acceptance are verifiable to anyone who cares enough to look, really look, at the world of people around them. You can observe how people treat others to see if they are tolerant or accepting. While we could go over every group and point out the differences between tolerance and acceptance, we need to concentrate on only one factor if we want to become the best we can be. That is how we feel.

If our feelings toward any one group or individual does not align with total acceptance, then we are only tolerating or perhaps just down right rejecting that group or individual. If we unwillingly work with someone, we are not accepting them. This does not mean everyone we meet will become our new best friend. What it does mean is that we accept that person into our circle to do the task at hand. That works whether it is at a job or at a meeting or in a neighborhood.

The better we can meet people on an even vibrational level, the better we will feel and the more aligned we are with our best self and gaining the desires we have in life.

In summing it up, we can view tolerance another way. We may simply put up with some people or situations until they change or until we are able to change them. Acceptance gives us a common ground that says, "It is all okay, and it doesn't need to change for anyone or any reason." This is the big difference.

THE VALUE OF ACCEPTANCE AND APPROVAL

"Acceptance is the greatest form of approval that we can ask for."

—Nancy Zimmerman

I am claiming this quote as mine. I researched to find whether I had read these words or something I felt within. While reading page after page of quotes about acceptance and approval, I learned a lot. I also learned that this is simply my take on the topic. If I have inadvertently stolen it from someone else, please correct me and know that I did not intend to do so. This quote sums up how I have always felt about acceptance for myself personally. When someone accepts me fully in all my states of chaotic behavior, I realize that they deeply care for and approve of me.

I was speaking with a young man I had just met. He has a great deal of artistic talent, and we were discussing his projects and where he was headed in the coming year. He had been doing a comic strip for the local newspaper for two or three years, but it had become a chore rather than a joy, so he decided to take his talent in a different direction and create his own characters in his own book. He told me that one of the defining factors that made creating the strip a chore came from one woman who continually put the strip down because he was writing about a single mother and her child. She kept telling him that he shouldn't do that because he couldn't relate, being a black male. After talking to him, I told him that because he was raised in a single parent home, he did have insight. He then said something extremely insightful for an accomplished young man of twenty-two. "I decided I didn't really need anyone to accept my work. I just decided to stay true to myself, and that would be acceptance enough. The strip was under guidelines of the newspaper, and my work is under my own guidelines. My guideline is to just have fun with it, and that is what I am able to do now."

Oh, to live in a world of such self-acceptance from such an early age. He will be a very successful artist, I believe. For the record, the young man is named Dee Parsons, and he is the creator of *Pen and Ink*, a story of a nineteen-year-old woman and her three-year-old sister. It is bright, witty, and very well done. In the prepublished edition I saw, guest illustrators had drawn their version of the characters.

This young man had accepted himself and his talent. As we talked, I could see many things that would create his success in addition to his talent. He talked about growing up in a small, conservative community in Indiana, where he had heard every racist remarks that could be made. As a young adult, he accepted that; he said he was now immune to the slurs. He accepted that some people are going to feel the way they feel and say what they will say. He knows already that it has nothing to do with him. He realizes that it is a reflection of how they feel about his skin color and nothing more.

Because of his intuitive acceptance of some of the behavior of others, he will be a great role model for young black children, especially young black males. There seems to be a shortage of black artists and authors, and this, he felt, was probably because of the lack of encouragement for this kind of talent as they were growing up. His talent was obviously encouraged, and he had a joy about his accomplishments. His goal is to share his gift, whether it be his art or his enthusiasm for life, and help others see that life needs to be fun. This is someone who is in the Vortex heading downstream, accepting all life has to offer.

The interesting part of this story is that I had titled this chapter and had written the first paragraph before I left to meet the young man for the first time. Our conversation led us to the perfect discussion to be shared in this chapter on acceptance and approval. This is another perfect example of how you accept life and it gives you what you need. It is a verification and a validation of the premise of the title. It enabled me to see further into the title and perhaps add to the quote: "Self-acceptance is all the approval we need."

When we jump from acceptance from others to self-acceptance, we get a great jump in our personal vibration. For years I needed the approval of others. I still like it when someone compliments me. I think we all enjoy the approval of others as a validation that we have made a good choice or have done well at a task. The problem arises when we need that approval to validate what we are doing. When we need the approval and validation from others, we lose that internal voice that is telling us we are okay as we are, the internal, vibrational intuition that led us to make the choice in the first place. If we don't get a verbal approval, we sometimes play a scenario that somehow we dropped the ball and made an error. This creates resistance to getting to our best self. When we can look in the mirror and not only approve but accept what we see, we take ourselves out of that "wobble" state and into terra firma.

I had published my first three Best Self books and a co-authored novel and novella as well as two of my children's books when I got a website designed. A person close to me was at my home using my washer and dryer because his was broken. When I asked if he would like to see my website, he said, "No, I am not interested in your little hobby." WOW... I realized that those three slurs were indicative of some problems that person had and had nothing to do with my writing. One: not interested; two: little (as in insignificant); and three: hobby—just a passing blip. I called him on it because it is one thing to not be interested, but quite another to dismiss someone's work. Even if I were to view my writing and publishing as a hobby, it would still be a hobby of which I am proud. I have worked hard to get my best work out there. To be dismissed so cavalierly and rudely was not something I would accept for myself.

I told the person that I felt he, perhaps, had issues that had nothing to do with me and he needed to look at his own life to see what needed to be fixed. The person took his clothes and left. I could not help but shake my head at the absurdity of what had taken place. All I could do was accept that he had some issues and hope the relationship was not damaged beyond repair. A couple of days later, the situation was revisited. While I accepted the rift, there had been a shift in how I perceived that person in relation to me. We are still in communication, but there is never going to be the same kind of ease there once was. I can accept that. If he ever reads this book, he might recognize himself and see this, but I doubt that will be an issue. He has determined my writing and thoughts are not important to him, and unless he changes his mind, that is just the way it will be. As you can tell, I am still writing, and it is still my hope that whoever picks up these books and reads them will be helped by what I have to say.

There was a time when this would have sent me into a downward spiral of self-doubt, but I have come to see that when we change our reaction to the voices of others, we literally change our entire vibrational frequency. When we make it our firm goal to feel good about everything in our lives, we find that it becomes easier and easier to shrug off the comments of others, to accept whatever they throw at us verbally and not let it affect our feelings. When we do not take it personally but look at it as the reflection of emotions they are having, we can accept this kind of discourse. This does not mean we have to like it, but we accept it for what it is—their view and only their view, which has nothing to do with us or our value.

WHAT HAPPENS TO OUR LIVES WHEN WE ACCEPT EVERYTHING?

"Our uniqueness, our individuality, and our life experience molds us into fascinating beings. I hope we can embrace that. I pray we may all challenge ourselves to delve into the deepest resources of our hearts to cultivate an atmosphere of understanding, acceptance, tolerance, and compassion. We are all in this life together."

—Linda Thompson

When accepting everything, we have to also include everyone. The above quote is correct when it says we are all in this life together. When we look at others in a way that does not accept them as they are, we are, in essence, making a judgment, usually one that has conditions to it. We are placing a value on an individual. When we place values on ourselves and deem ourselves to be unworthy in some aspect, we are said to have low self-esteem

Self-esteem is often likened to self-acceptance, but it is different. Self-esteem rises as does the value we place on ourselves regarding certain aspects. Self-acceptance allows us to embrace everything, all facets of ourselves, not just the positive things. Self-acceptance embraces the weaknesses and limitations we perceive as well as the more positive attributes. And that acceptance means we don't put conditions or qualifications on whether something is worthy of being accepted; we just accept it all.

Tremendous growth appears when we look at the parts of ourselves that we cannot accept. When I look at my body and see its perfection of creation rather than a size that advertising moguls tell us is unacceptable, I can begin to accept it more fully. When I realize that I am not fat but rather I have fat, I can agree that everyone has fat. I can then accept that I have more fat than some people and less fat than others. What was unacceptable slowly begins to become more acceptable until one day I realize that my body is okay. I have accepted it fully. If I look at parts of it and believe it needs to be smaller or firmer or larger or whatever I think it needs to be, then I have not reached total, unconditional acceptance and love of my self and my body.

Acceptance of everything is a form of love. True self-acceptance is the love for ourselves that I thought might need its own book. Now I realize that fully accepting ourselves is that love.

I will run down some experiences to show you how acceptance opens up how you view things. As Eckhart Tolle explains time and time again (and I will paraphrase this),

> We must accept the now. To do otherwise would be foolish because there is no other time but now. If we push against things and say, "no, I don't accept that," it won't change anything.

Think about it. Has cursing the weather ever changed it? Has bemoaning a traffic jam ever made the cars go any faster? If we don't like what someone has to say, have they ever changed their minds, even after we have argued and argued? If they did, was it worth the effort it took and chaos it caused? Was it a real change, or was it just a nod so you would quit badgering them?

Looking at unacceptable things and turning them around in your mind so you can not only tolerate them but truly accept them is a simple matter of changing your thoughts about the people or issues you are not willing to accept. One of the areas of concern can be in how we deal with relationships.

There are several facets of relationships that need acceptance. There is the time of the relationship where one person cares and the other person doesn't. You cannot control how another person feels about you. It is just that simple. I have spent hours wondering why someone doesn't care for me as much as they once seemed to care. When all is said and done, does it really matter? The fact is that they don't. Period. It doesn't matter why, but the longer we hold onto that, the more we stay in a place of resistance and lower vibration. Then we wind up shutting off the flow of good things coming to us. We are not in alignment with others who might love us. We are not in alignment to receive other things that we are hoping to have in our lives. In essence, we have put up a barrier while we sit and worry about something that was here and now is not. Back away from this. Look at it as though someone else was facing that. In my case, people had tried, gently, to tell me that I was being held back in my achievement because of the limitations that another individual was putting on me. I kept hoping this person would step up as he had said he wanted to and would be part of the team. He didn't. He backed away further. He backed out entirely. I was left with a mess to clean up. I took the steps I need to and did the work I needed to do to get myself extricated from the situation. It was a lengthy process. I tried to get him to discuss the outcome, but my messages were ignored.

I was not hurt and I was not really angry, but I was not yet ready to accept that the association was over. We had worked well together. We had shared many good times, and I had bountiful good memories of working with him on several projects. It was then that I realized that it didn't matter where he was or why he had left; it would never be the same if he were to return to the project. He could have come to me the day it hit me, and I would have told him I no longer wanted to work with him. My trust was gone. I had these wonderful memories, and because of the work we did together, I had accomplished things that were originally out of my skill set but were now comfortable. I could take that skill set and apply it to work that was solely mine without compromise. I could extend and expand my platform in a way that I would not have been able to if I had continued working with him because I was spending so much time doing work that he was letting go. I suddenly realized that I was free to be a more productive, creative me, and I accepted that the association had reached its due date and was over.

We do not suddenly wake up and have everything be acceptable. Sometimes acceptance comes in bits and pieces like it did over about a ten-month period in the example above. Sometimes it was better and sometimes it was worse, but in the end, it was all okay. I was able to see the good through the not-so-good, sort it out, and take the best away from the association. I then was able to accept the bad parts as being okay because they led to the good parts that I still own.

One also has to accept that sometimes the timing is just not right. In relationships, one party may not be ready at the same time or with the same intensity that the other party is. It will only bring you down vibrationally if you do not accept it. This does not mean that it will never be right; it may be right with this person at a later time, or it may be right with another person altogether. I think about people who marry others and then later in life get back with people they were with earlier in their lives. Accept the timing. Doing so will keep you vibrationally sound and will allow other opportunities to flow to you.

I wrote the paragraph above and put it to bed last evening. This morning I had an appointment with a guest I will be having on my radio talk show Friday evening. We discussed timing in relationships. There are times when people meet and think they have found "the one" only to realize they haven't. The problem is that they often find the true soul connection after they have married. This causes problems for everyone, and it is too bad when it happens. To be true to yourself is a difficult task at times. Accepting that things work out in divine time helps us adjust to events that don't turn out as we expect or hope.

Once more we look at expectations. When we expect certain outcomes, we are more often than not disappointed. Accepting the outcome, regardless of what it is, helps us get through the trials we experience. We cannot push against what is happening. That will cause more conflict. When we push back, whatever we are pushing against becomes our focus. The subject of our focus then takes a larger place in the whole picture and becomes a more dominant concern. When we simply allow the events to unfold as they will and reserve any judgment about them, acceptance is easier.

THE ROLE JUDGMENT PLAYS
IN ACCEPTANCE

"The mental suffering you create is always some form of non-acceptance, some form of unconscious resistance to what is. On the level of thought, the resistance is some form of judgment. The intensity of the suffering depends on the degree of resistance to the present moment."

–Eckhart Tolle

The role of judgment is significant. When we judge others, we are reflecting our judgment of ourselves. As humans, we project from a place of insecurity. We judge others in order to elevate ourselves. When we are confident and accepting of ourselves, we have no reason to judge others. We have no reason to look for ways to tear them down so we can feel better.

Once you begin judging, it comes back upon you and others will judge you. When you recognize your judgmental thoughts and actions, you can then choose to accept people and their differences. Once you do that, people will stop judging you and accept you. This may not happen overnight, but if you remove the expectations of time, it will happen.

When people do judge you, don't take it personally. That is one of the Four Agreements by don Miguel Ruiz. When we take judgment personally, we give it power, and we tend to want to retaliate. Our ego wants to elevate itself. If we take nothing personally but just accept what others say, we diffuse the situation and make the statement inert. We remove its ability to harm us. We have accepted it as an opinion and have accepted that it poses no harm.

When we look at nonjudgment as one of the goals of acceptance, we see that several factors play a part. We have discussed accepting as it relates to our differences and accepting those. We have looked at factors that lead us to judgment. Let us now look at how the three interact and how we can take out the judgment, ignore the differences, and fully accept whatever is happening.

Because I am in a much better state of self-acceptance of my body, I will use that to illustrate what I am talking about. I was young when my mother first told me, "You would be so pretty if only you would lose weight." I was probably about ten when she said this. When that statement is processed in a young girl's mind, it comes through in several ways. It says to her that she is not pretty because she weighs "too much"—and "too much" isn't even defined. Is it two pounds or twenty pounds. What is "too much?" Then there is the word "pretty." What does that mean? To a young girl heading into puberty, it means she is fat and ugly. Now I know realistically that was not the message my mother intended, but it was the message I received and carried with me until recently.

As I grew up being overweight, I knew I was not totally ugly. I knew I had some redeeming features. I knew I was not too ugly to have friends, but to make myself feel better, I looked at girls my age. If they had a body that fit into the kinds of clothes I would like to have worn but did not come in my size, I would find a way to judge them. I would tell myself that they were not smart. That they had ugly hair or eyes or some other feature. I would judge them in any way I could so I would not feel the hurt of being "fat and ugly."

As a young woman, I lost much weight, but I still saw myself as fat. I did, however, quit making the judgments I had as a young girl because I could now shop for clothes I liked and I liked the reflection I saw in the mirror. I married, had a couple of children, and got divorced.

In an effort to avoid the hurt of a relationship that I was afraid would fail, I ate and gained weight as a defense. I then began the judgments again. I kept this up to varying degrees for years. I did not openly and cruelly judge, but I would find things wrong with almost everyone, even my friends.

As I began to grow in my awareness of myself, I realized what I had been doing. I found that as I gave up judging others, I felt less judgmental of myself. I would catch myself judging people's looks, something I had never been aware I was doing before. As I worked on this, my judgment of what I perceived as flaws in my own looks became less severe. I am not going to suggest that this has gone away entirely. I still look at myself some days and see wrinkles that I didn't notice the day before. Then there are days that I don't even notice the wrinkles. What I notice is a direct reflection of how I am feeling about myself in other ways, and it manifests in what I see in the mirror.

When the awareness came through, the judgment slowed down. When my judgment of others slowed down, the self-judgment eased. When the self-judgment eased, I had less reason to judge others, and my self-worth went up. While judgment can throw us into a downward spiral of negative emotion, the reverse is also true. As we get into a state of nonjudgment we realize we were judging others because we thought that they were judging us. In essence, we were judging ourselves and projecting our perceived faults and flaws onto others, usually people we didn't even know. I would make assumptions about people to negate my inadequate feelings of self-worth.

As you can see, there is such a component of acceptance to include nonjudgment. Many factors can hinder our acceptance of situations, and it is up to us to sort those out, deal with them, and stop them from lowering our vibrations. This is not as difficult when we accept that we are vibrational beings; wherever our vibrations are, we are attracting situations at that level.

When we let the trials of life pull us down, more and more things come into our lives that are of that lower frequency. The friend I previously mentioned can see, hear, and feel frequencies in others. She has had this gift she was three years old. She was able to see rainbows around people and did not realize that not everyone saw these rainbows (aka auras). As she progressed through her life, it was difficult for her to adjust when she was able to see those who had passed as well as angels. She could bring forth energy and see where relationships had gone wrong. She is an amazing person in her ability to work with energy. What she does is not unique because she follows the innate intuition she was born with. We are all born with it to a degree, but not the degree she possesses. She works with people to teach them how to use their intuitive power. I was at an introductory seminar of hers, and as she began to talk, I realized that much of what I have been writing has been along the same vein. I do not possess the same abilities, but my books reflect different ways you can get in touch and hone your vibrations.

As the seminar neared an end and people began asking questions, she looked over at me and encouraged me, knowing I had something to say. I simply related that as I was listening, I was no longer surprised that she and I had met and were planning a project or two together because we were working on the same energy wave, just coming at it from different directions.

FINAL THOUGHTS ON ACCEPTANCE

Before we take acceptance one step further, I want to stress one more time that you should use those vibrational tools and get yourself to the highest vibrations. Tune that frequency into those things that will bring you peace and joy. Live each moment of the day in that joy and appreciation for everything that shows up, knowing that the Universe is directing and orchestrating events and situations so your desires come to you. The only thing you have to remember is to stay out of your own way. You will invariably let negative thoughts creep into your mind and disallow what would and could rightfully be yours. We give "yes, I want it" and "no, I don't want it" messages to the guiding Universe hundreds of times when we waver in our dreams and goals.

We need to develop a fearless attitude. Develop the "I am and I can" attitude and do not doubt yourself. Sit back and relax, knowing that you have accepted whatever is coming your way as part of the divine unfolding of your dreams. Be eager to see, and thank the Universe for whatever shows up, knowing that more is on the way.

I want to close this chapter with something that I found to be very helpful. It is on my bulletin board in front of my desk where I can read it several times daily.

This is from Thom Rutledge, an author and psychotherapist:

To accept something does not mean you like it.
It means you know you can't change it.
It means you know you need to find another way.
It means you know it is time to let go.
It means you know it is time to move on.
It means you are ready to discover what is next.
Are you ready?

LOVING

YOUR

BEST SELF

THE FINAL TENET

When I began writing my first book, *Embracing Your Best Self,* I had one goal in mind: to organize the myriad bits of information I was garnering from other sources in a way that I could understand. I accepted some of these bits of information and rejected others as I read and studied. I realized that to assimilate everything into one understandable work, I should write a book. Little did I realize that the work was just beginning.

When I began to be complacent, I began writing the second, then the third book. They came together rather easily from the standpoint of knowing what was next. The premise of the third came while I was still working on the second one, *Confronting Your Best Self.*

As I wrote that book, I knew that to maintain your best self in any way would require a balancing of mind, body, and spirit. The third book, *Balancing Your Best Self,* was an accumulation of how I was beginning to live my life on a daily basis.

When it was done, I knew enough about love and acceptance that I realized a person would have to accept the reality of their daily life for the balancing to take hold. They would have to accept it so thoroughly that it would become a part of who they were. It could not be half-hearted positivity. It would have to be an all-consuming acceptance of life, regardless of whatever harsh situations one was faced with.

I contemplated grotesque scenarios as I wrote about acceptance. I thought about losing everything. Could I accept that? Could I accept homelessness, loss of friends and family? Could I accept a friend's refusal to stand by me? I put myself as close to those situations as I could imagine, and through it all, I realized that whatever life threw at me, I could not only get through it but accept it as the hand of the divine source guiding me to greater things. It was not easy with some of the scenarios I plotted, but once I did that, I knew I was ready to write *Accepting Your Best Self*.

One of the repeating themes in all of the reading I did was not only the importance of acceptance of everything but also self-acceptance. Then, going further, the ultimate charge was to learn to truly love yourself. This one stymied me until just recently when I was given the greatest gift of all, the ability to not only understand loving myself, but the ability to actually do it.

With this in mind, I wrote the last part of the book, *Accepting Your Best Self.* When you learn to love yourself, you have reached the apex of accepting your best self, and you only have to continue to live from this point to begin to attract those things you desire. You also push acceptance to a new level when you allow things you have avoided, like pain and hurt, into your life. You will live a life so fully connected to your Source that all things will be given to you. You will find that if something is not forthcoming quickly, you will be okay with that because you are seeing the value of yourself.

Many factors determine how we see ourselves. We will begin with the view that society puts on us and has for generations. Because societal norming occurs through the generations, what we think of as normal is not normal.

We are created in the image of our Source. The same stardust that created the Universe is in us; indeed we are made of the same building blocks you will find in stardust. When it is said, ashes to ashes and dust to dust, it is literal in the interpretation. We are eternal nonphysical energy making a physical appearance in these "pods" we call our bodies. Our bodies are prepared for us by the female of the species, and society then determines that there are special feelings associated with this. We need time to nurture the pod so it can survive on its own. That time varies, and as society changes, so does that time. At one time, young men and women married at the age of fourteen or fifteen. It was prudent to do so because the desire to procreate began at that age. It was also a time when families needed additional help to make a living, and it was simply a convenient way for families to live.

As society moved from a rural to an urban existence and as men were conscripted to go off to wars and women were left to do the factory work, the mores of society changed. Today we are reaping what we sowed many years ago. We have a society whereby women no longer are dependent on a man for their livelihood, so they are becoming more selective. When we consider these facts, we see that the average age at which to marry has grown to about the age of twenty-eight.

As we view the societal norms and apply them to our lives, we can see that if a child of fifteen were to marry now, we would be appalled, even though at one time it was the norm. What is acceptable at one time is not necessarily acceptable at another.

We experience a certain kind of love when we find someone we want as a mate. It is based on many factors, which do not always include love. When we reach an age where we want to have a mate, it is usually to procreate and reproduce. We each look for many characteristics when choosing a partner. Although this is a book about loving our best selves, we need to understand the scope of love.

The Sanskrit language has ninety-six ways to express love; in Ancient Persian, there were eighty. The Greek language has three, but the English language has only one. Because of this lack of vocabulary about one of the all-consuming emotions we all experience, we are understandably confused when we express this emotion. Love is such an immense emotion that to cram all of the nuances into one word can be rather painful.

From the beginning of our lives, we seek acceptance and love. Acceptance and love are so fully intertwined that as we begin learning we make the mistake of thinking they are the same thing. We think that if someone accepts us, that means they love us, and if they say they love us, that means they accept us. That is not always true. There are countless times when love is expressed verbally and shown to be something entirely different when time is applied to the situation.

I grew up in what I thought was a loving family. If my parents approved of us, their love was expressed through their kind words. If, however, we "misbehaved" according to their rules, love and the expression of love was withheld. This is how I was brought up to think of love. My parents' love was based on our actions, not unconditional love. Most parents, if not all, seem to place some conditions on their expression of love to their children. They believe they need to show their disapproval and do so through the withdrawal of affection. To a young child, this equates to a withdrawal of love itself. This gives a skewed version of what love is.

We grow up, meet someone, and fall in love. We love based on how we learned to love and be loved. When we meet someone whose idea of love is like ours, we match. This is why you find people in abusive situations. We wonder why a man would treat a woman like that and why a woman would allow it. Very often it is because those behaviors were imprinted upon them when they were young.

You also have instances where there would be bad treatment, but one party or the other will not continue in the same pattern. In those instances, children learn what they will *not* tolerate or how they will *not* act because they saw that behavior rejected by the other parent.

So we have models of how to love from the time we are born. They may be good models or they may be bad models, but sometimes they have nothing to do with the real emotion of love. Love is love. It does not ask behaviors of us. When we learn to love unconditionally, we cannot help loving another.

I will use the example of a person I love unconditionally. I must because he has treated me badly. We acknowledged a soul connection when we met and began a friendship that had high vibrations. We began working on a project, and we both experienced a great deal of positive energy and enjoyment. I thought the friendship would last. After our work was done and we both went to other things, I viewed the relationship as important enough to keep in touch; he did not. When I last saw him with a friend of his whom I knew, his friend spoke to me, but he did not. I still puzzle over that, but because of the work I have done on myself in writing this series, I was able to release any angst and disappointment fairly quickly. I separated the behavior from the energy. There will always be a connection between the two of us, whether he speaks to me or not. I have accepted that. I know that love is there, and it just is. I also have the life I have now because of events that happened to us when we were working together. I took risks I would not have taken and met people I would not have met. He prepared me for people I would meet and events I would experience with his unconditional love and support for the time he freely gave it. What a gift it was!

When you can remove the emotions that relationships create and view the blessings they provided for at least a portion of your life, it all settles into that area of "divine timing." We were destined to meet. We were destined to become friends and to question how far that friendship would go and how long it would last. I taught him things, and he taught me things. I also have to accept that some purpose was served in the way it ended. And perhaps it has only ended temporarily so there is room for other things; maybe he will be one of the relationships that ebb and flow in my life. These people are meant to come in and out of our lives with more than one lesson to learn.

It took time for me to release this friend. For one thing, it took time to realize that I needed to release the relationship. I had not seen the depth of his withdrawal for a while. When I did, I began releasing a bit at a time even though I still wanted to hold on to it. That is yet another aspect of love to be discussed.

When we love others, we often become possessive of their love. We want to be their only love, their best friend, but it doesn't work that way. We have much love to offer others, and there are many different kinds of love. The love we have for our parents is much different than the love we have for our brothers and sisters. Love for our aunts, uncles, and cousins is different still. We have friends we love.

When we have spouses and children, those are loved differently also.

When we look for romantic love from a friend and they offer only friendship, we have to decide what we are going to do. Many people decide that if they can't have the romance, they will look elsewhere and forego the friendship. That is conditional love. It is based on something outside ourselves and does not comeg from within. This happened to a friend. She and a friend of hers realized that they both cared for each other deeply, and it caught them off guard. Her friend put the brakes on it. She understood. The timing was not right. They had agreed that their friendship would always have top priority. He thought she would turn her back on the relationship and he would lose her. Luckily for them both, the lines of communication had been established, and they both cared enough about each other that they are still friends to this day. At some point, if the timing is ever right, it will be a beautiful romance. They have already established their unconditional love for each other. Words do not need to be spoken for them both to know this.

When you go through all of the steps to accept others, you are preparing yourself for love. When you begin to accept yourself, you set yourself up for that same love. When you do not put conditions on others, you remove any judgment. When you no longer judge others, you see that no one is judging you. When no one judges you, you quit judging yourself. When you quit judging yourself, you are in a place of acceptance. That is when you begin to love.

When the day comes that we can look in the mirror and truly like the person we are, the person we have become, and embrace the person looking back at us as being a great individual, we have reached a place of loving ourselves.

HOW TO LOVE WHAT WE
DO NOT LOVE

I have heard about the concept of loving ourselves my entire life. As a young girl, I was encouraged to love myself, but I really did not understand it. My family did not show affection easily. I grew up having my needs met: I had a roof over my head, warm clothes in the winter, and food on the table. This was what I equated with love. During the time I grew up, this was how love was expressed by most families. When I was in my twenties and attending college to become a teacher, I discovered that there was a trend to be concerned about children's psyches so they would grow up perhaps more well adjusted than we had.

As political correctness entered the scene, people were encouraged to allow children to express themselves and never tell them they were not "good enough." Because of this, we began to raise children who developed a feeling of entitlement. But I digress again. The divide about what was good parenting and what was not good parenting widened. What did we want our children to absorb as they grew into adulthood? While some children felt like anything they did should be considered acceptable, even more children began feeling like they were always falling short of the goals.

As we grow up, we learn behavior. From the crib onward, we learn how to maneuver in society. Babies learn behavior. In that respect we are like any other animals. We mimic the behavior we see from the adults of our species. Everything the human animal becomes is learned from those around us. It works this way whether good or bad. When we enter the world, we are closely connected with the Source from which we came. If you watch babies, they often appear to be reaching out to someone, but as adults we see no one. They do. Think of the times that your children professed to have "imaginary friends." Adults will tell the child that they can't be seeing "someone" because the adults can't. However, there is more and more evidence that young children indeed can see images of those who have passed. We all possess an intuition and an ability to see angel spirits and spirit guides. It is often programmed out of us as we grow older because it has been programmed out of the adults we are around.

When we are told that we don't see what we see, that we don't hear what we hear, and that we don't feel what we feel, we begin to lose touch with our intuition. It is critical to have a good sense of intuition if we are to accept and love ourselves at an early age. We are born to love. We accept everyone until we are shown a reason not to. Even when people are mistreated, it is often difficult to turn away from them and discount the love we have. It is my personal belief that as long as there is love between two individuals, there will not be abuse. When you love someone, you want the very best for them, and you do nothing that diminishes their enjoyment of life.

Although it is our own responsibility to be happy, we often look for love from someone else to make us happy. When we put our happiness on the shoulders of someone else, we are placing a responsibility on them that is inherently unfair. I had a friend from Canada tell me that for us to expect one person to meet one hundred percent of our needs one hundred percent of the time is an unrealistic expectation of anyone. He was one hundred percent correct. Because of the nature of love and the nature of our expectations of others, we constantly find ourselves disappointed both in love and with others.

Because we become disappointed with the love of others, we skew our vision of what love is. We think that if a person acted in a certain way, that would represent love. I have seen women go after men so they would have a date on a Saturday night. It did not matter to these women how the man treated them; they simply wanted to be seen with a man so everyone would think they were loved. I have seen men marry beautiful but cold women so they could parade them in front of their friends in an effort to boost their own ego. I have seen nice men be treated like their love is worth nothing to the woman they are married to. I do not understand these behaviors.

I do not fall in love easily. I think because I do not "fall in love" like many women do, it has played a role in loving myself. The men I have loved, aside from family members, have invited me into their space first. I have observed and, in a couple of instances, been totally caught off guard by the man's interest. In loving myself, I look for lovable, observable characteristics in myself. I know now that is not how love operates. I know that when we look at every man and woman with kindness, compassion, and, yes, love, we get a different view of love. We do not see it as a narrowly defined word, but rather an all-encompassing feeling. We begin to look at oppressed people with love. We see others as worthy and lovable because just in viewing them we realize our connection.

When we change the way we think about love, our entire world shifts. We no longer think about falling in love with someone, we simply love. When we do that, love comes to us. Potential partners have come into my life when I was not looking for anyone or anything to complete me. It has happened when I have been confident and secure in who I am and what I am doing. Because I have not needed anyone, I see with different eyes.

When you begin to look at all of those around you with love, your judgment falls to the side. If there is no judgment of others, you are easier on yourself. You realize that nothing matters but the essence of others. If you have been following my other writing, you will be aware that I believe we all share a conscious connection. In that connection, we are the same. The Universal Source that creates is the nonphysical self. In that nonphysical self is the Universal Source. All religions understand that the source of creation cannot be divided. If that is the case, then there is no division. That source is reaching out like seven billion "fingers" into the pod of humanity where we exist.

I find this concept fascinating. We are all source energy expressing ourselves as individual physical entities, each with different fingerprints, hair color, eyes, ears, and brains to use. We are free to move around as "individuals" with but connectedness.

If we are all connected and we have developed the compassion to "do unto others as you would have done unto you," is there any way we are not worthy of that compassionate love ourselves? The only answer to that question is a resounding, "NO!"

Growing up, I loved to argue. I honed that trait to an artform. My father once told me I should be a lawyer, but I was not encouraged to do that. I was told to go to school and become a teacher (something I had wanted to do since I was always playing school). My mother told me I would argue with a post, given the chance. She also told me if I wanted to move something, it might as well move because I wouldn't stop until it did. I look at these statements now and see them as strengths. When I was young, they were said in a way to let me know that my thoughts and behaviors were not acceptable. To argue questioned authority, their authority, and that was not acceptable behavior.

When I argued with my parents, there was no room for discussion. I was being disrespectful. I was questioning authority. I needed to be taught this was not the way I should behave, and some kind of chore was issued so I could think about how I had behaved. It did not stop me from arguing, and it did not stop me from gaining approval if I behaved as they wanted and expected me to and having their approval withheld if I did not. When I was engaged, my father once told me that I had better learn to keep my mouth shut because he and my mother had to "put up with me and my mouth" but my husband would not have to. These kinds of statements were not deliberately meant to be unkind, but they were unkind. They created a sense of insecurity about how my behavior and my lovability were intertwined.

When the people who were supposed to love me the most sent such inconsistent messages, it was no wonder I was confused over what love was. And it was no wonder that I could not love myself. I stumbled through relationships after my divorce with the same insecurity I had felt before my divorce. I eventually gave up on having a relationship and withdrew from interacting with others to what degree I could. If I did not put myself out there, I could not be rejected and could not be made to feel unlovable.

As I began reading and becoming more aware of the true nature of what we are, it opened up avenues of understanding that I had not been exposed to. Much of the dogma and "rules" that I had grown up with were uncovered as necessary for me to question. This gave me a chance to question without argument. I found there was no right and wrong in my questions. I was finding my own answers. I learned that my answers were as good as anyone's about how my life would unfold. In this I found a great deal of peace and joy. I found happiness for the first time in my life. I found that happiness from within. I was doing what gave me the highest frequency in life. I smiled more, I laughed more, and I sought out others. I was learning to love myself.

As I realized that all I had to do was get out of my own way and treat others with kindness and compassion, I was receiving this from other sources. I learned to give of myself to others in some way, even if it were only in a smile. I realized that this was a form of love, love for my fellow beings. I still did not understand how I could love myself.

I was still using the paradigm I had always used. I was judging myself from a point of egoic concerns, concerns based on others, on advertising what was good and normal, and on things outside myself. I then began writing *Accepting Your Best Self.* After I began this book almost two years ago, I took several breaks in the writing of it. I would write a few thousand words and then stop for a couple of months. When I finished another project, I would pick back up and write some more after reading and rewriting what I had already written. I would then write a few thousand more words and collect more thoughts, only to begin another project and stop the work when I got to a place of puzzlement. This happened four or five times over those two years.

I realized that if I was ever going to get the book written, I needed to make a concentrated effort to get my thoughts on paper. I had another project in the Best Self series that was dependent on the completion of that book. I took a weekend to write and rewrite what was already down on paper. I moved some things around and explained other things and then set about to complete the work.

When I was nearing what I felt to be the end, I realized I had begun to truly accept myself. I was aware of some of the limitations and frustrations that I used to have. I had adjusted my thinking and viewed those limitations through another lens. I also had learned to accept those characteristics that I had previously viewed as flaws with a different eye. I now saw that I was simply experiencing more steps in the process of acceptance. There was nothing wrong with where I was in the process. I abandoned the idea of "it will be better when I get over there." I knew that where I was right now was the best place to be or I would not be there.

The realization came slowly, but the more I wrote, the clearer it became. I felt my vibrational health rise, and I became more and more excited about finishing the work and planned for the continuation in some other offerings. In my excitement, I found people who were supportive of my talents and efforts.

We live in an inclusive world. We cannot invite something in and then put a hand out and say, "Wait, no, I don't want that." Whatever we invite in, good or bad, becomes a part of our lives. It was a time when I began to focus differently. I found doors opening that I had not realized were there. Doors were not closing on me; rather, I was opting to go down different halls to find new opportunities. I was thinking outside the box, and I was listening to the suggestions of those who were sent by spirit guides to help me.

One of the most serious issues for me has been that of relationships and love. I found compassion for others and was treating myself more kindly, but I had questions, which hypnosis has helped me with. The energy within me and within others let me know I was treasured and loved. When I made the realization that I did not know how to respond to having someone love me, I was told by an intuitive, "It is because you have never felt worthy of love until now. You know your own worth, and you now know you are worthy of the love of another person." In that instance I realized that I did know that now, and I was ready to open my heart to love. The greatest source of that love is the Source that is inside me. It is the Source that is inside all of us. With that realization came the peace that my love for myself was enough, and in that knowing, I knew that when love from an outside source came I would truly be ready for it.

Once you accept love for yourself, you understand the complete circle of acceptance.

You are free to look around and see the world through the eyes of the Source from which you are created. You know the lessons, and you are ready for more. I am not sure what "more" is, but I know I am on the precipice of finding out more and more about what I am here for. Each day is an adventure regardless of what happens. I accept everything that is happening *now* as being a part of the divine unfolding for my life. I know there are people who will be on this journey with me. I have met some of them, and they are already with me. Some I have yet to meet, and I find that exciting.

I had no idea when I began writing these books about five years ago that the journey would take me to the heights it has. The valleys were not as low because of what I began to understand. There will be at least one more book in this series at the adult level, *Celebrating Your Best Self.* I have been asked to write a series for elementary, middle school, and high school students to help them navigate life earlier and more easily. It is in the planning stages.

I am now ready to take this series to the only place I know to take it, and that is to share it with others. I plan to create a guidebook that will accompany this series. While the series is called *Discovering Your Best Self,* the guidebook will be entitled *Creating Your Best Self*. In it you will be charged with discovering *how* to create *your* best self.

This will be a journey you and I take together as I continue to unfold more and more of this beautiful life we have been given. For more information on my writing, my journey, and an online workshop and class I will be offering in the near future, go to www.nzbestself.com. Feel free to contact me with any questions. It is all a journey, and it is the journey that is so very beautiful. The destination is the bonus.

Namaste,

Nancy

www.ingramcontent.com/pod-product-compliance
Lightning Source LLC
LaVergne TN
LVHW051503080426
835509LV00017B/1895